POSTBUS COUNTRY

GLIMPSES OF RURAL SCOTLAND

POSTBUS COUNTRY

GLIMPSES OF RURAL SCOTLAND

JOAN BURNIE

Photographs

DOUGLAS CORRANCE

CANONGATE PRESS

First published in Great Britain in 1994 by
Canongate Press Ltd,
14 Frederick Street,
Edinburgh EH2 2HB.

The publishers gratefully acknowledge the support of Royal Mail Scotland
and Northern Ireland in publishing this book.

ISBN 0 86241 484 9

British Library Cataloguing-in-Publication Data
A catalogue record for this book is available on request
from the British Library.

Designed by Almond Design
Printed and bound by Imago Publishing Ltd,
Thame Oxfordshire
Colour separations by DOT Gradations, Chelmsford.

CONTENTS

FOREWORD

" We couldn't do without it!". As I travel round Scotland I hear this time and time again from our customers who rely on the Postbus. It sums up how important the service is to those living in remote communities who may have no other form of public transport.

It is a service of which we are immensely proud. It fits well with our mission and values and allows us to offer added value to customers who receive mail to their door no matter how remote their location.

The fact that the service is here at all today is a great tribute to the lateral thinking of those who over the past twenty five years managed our distribution operations in Scotland; their innovation helped them think beyond the obvious to discover a better way of combining our operations with a new service.

The Postbus would not be the same without its drivers. The affection with which the service is held in the passengers' hearts is a tribute to them, their enthusiasm, commitment and professionalism.

I would also like to dedicate this book to those who have played a great part in providing the inspiration for the postbus service. In particular to Trevor Carpenter, who had the vision of what the service could be; to Jim Hall, for translating this vision into a reality and to Ian Cruickshank, who with his indomitable personality and passion for the Highlands has continued to develop the service.

My thanks to you all.

John Mackay,
Director and General Manager,
Royal Mail Scotland and Northern Ireland

CHAPTER ONE

POSTBUS COUNTRY

There was a silver wedding in the summer of 1993. The postbus service in Scotland, which joined Royal Mail and passengers together in June 1968, celebrated its first twenty-five years. Twenty five years of postbuses, those red Land-Rovers, Sherpas and estate cars, driving into and becoming part of places too easily and readily overlooked by the rest of us and the busy world. In that time, its one pioneering postbus has grown to more than 140, which between them annually travel 2.8 million miles and carry 80,000 passengers.

And of course an awful lot more – the morning milk and papers, the daily bread and messages, flowers for a bride and chocolates for a remembered mother on her birthday, the prescriptions from doctors and vets for their rural patients, all cheerfully heaved in along with other occasionally less conventional cargo, both animal and vegetable, the quick and, at least once, the dead.

The initial Scottish journey took place in June 1968, travelling the few short miles between Dunbar and Innerwick via Spott, where Molly Lafferty

The first Scottish postbus sets out in 1968.

grasped her shopping bag and heaved herself aboard for the first time —
twenty-five years on, she still regularly claims her Monday morning window
seat. But the postbus service as a whole did not really begin with that red
Morris van turned instantly into a bus with seven hastily added seats. Nor did
it even begin in Scotland. Nor in Wales, where a service between Llanidloes
and Llangurig ran for a full seventeen months before the Scottish experiment.

Both – along with another couple of routes in Devon and the Lake District
– were in response to the Jack Report of 1961 (official reports then as now
take a great deal of time grinding through the mills of government) which had
examined the decline of public transport in rural areas and recommended the
Austrian and Swiss solution of marrying passengers and post.

One John Palmer, the Cameron MacIntosh of his day and impresario of the
main theatre in Bath, had reached the same, rather obvious conclusion almost
200 years previously. Like many a customer before and since of the mail, Mr
Palmer was not pleased by late deliveries. So in 1782 he buttonholed his Prime
Minister, William Pitt, and put before him the grand plan – that the

stagecoaches, which on the whole kept to their timetables, should take up post as well as passengers. Two years later – bureaucracy was, perhaps, not quite as bloated in those days – the first stage-and-mail coach ran between Bristol and London, taking in Bath, and no doubt Mr Palmer's thanks and vote, on the way. The spread of the service northwards seemed inevitable, and the Great North Road to Edinburgh got the new coach service in the summer of 1786.

Horse-power (four or six stout drays in harness, managing a maximum twelve miles an hour) could achieve some surprising results: Edinburgh to Aberdeen saw 134 miles covered in just over fourteen hours at its fastest. But within a few years they could not compete with the new railways' iron steeds which effortlessly ate up forty and more miles every hour. It was the time of the great railway rush when companies began and finished lines almost daily, and soon there was hardly a village or hamlet without its station or halt.

Increasingly, from 1830 on, the bulk of the mail was taken by train, at least to the large town termini until, in 1898, the last mail coach ran and post and passengers officially divorced. However, on economic grounds, and in places

The legendary Molly Lafferty and friend. Molly was the Postbus' first Scottish passenger on the initial service between Dunbar and Spott.

untouched by railways, on islands and the remoter countryside, there were and still are private firms delivering under contract both mail and people, although these ad hoc services invariably (and unlike today's postbuses) gave priority to the latter rather than the former.

And that, more or less, was that. Until the 1960s, by which time many of those Victorian lines of hope and glory had declined. They, in their turn, had, like the old stagecoaches, become transport dinosaurs and were equally doomed. By the time Lord Beeching had swung his scythe through them, there was not, particularly in Scotland, an awful lot of working railway line left. On the other hand, the mail was expanding. Its red vehicles were on every road and track, delivering to every urban house and rural home and farm. It seemed, at least to the Jack Report if not to those in power, that the time was right for passengers and post to be reconciled.

Yet those first tentative services were initially judged uneconomic, and the Post Office saw no future in the idea. At least in England. But in 1971, north of the border, Trevor Carpenter, who had been appointed Chairman of the Scottish Postal Board, and his Operations Controller, James Hall, thought rather differently.

They looked again at the accounts on their solitary Dunbar route and discovered that the postbus may have been red-coloured but was definitely running in the black, thanks to recently won contracts to carry goods for local businesses, passenger and transport grants. Of great importance too was the affection customers felt for it; in the jargon, postbuses were user-friendly.

So began an immediate expansion. The second service was started in Skye in 1972, when the private contractor who had run a post and passenger bus between Elgol and Broadford retired. Others followed rapidly, especially in the Highlands and Islands. By the mid 1970s there were eighty-four routes covering a million and a half miles every year and carrying 100,000 passengers. Peter Reid and George Thomson were instrumental in actively identifying new routes in Scotland's most remote areas: Peter worked tirelessly as Head Postmaster in Lerwick and Dumfries, while George enthusiastically expanded the service in the islands, where he robustly defended the postbus at a public hearing on Barra when the Royal Mail was challenged by another operator. George eventually moved to Inverness to take over from the late and certainly magnificently-named Reuben Appleyard.

Every time there was a new postbus, Reuben organised a very good party indeed, for it was always an event to be celebrated in style, with Lord Lieutenants, MPs, Provosts, councillors, and even the press in attendance. But those days are long gone. Bus deregulation in 1986 and political time, tide and emphasis, together with the other far-reaching changes in both Post Office and Royal Mail businesses, have moved the postbus service very firmly into a modern world which no longer hands out many free meals. When in 1992 the route was opened from Fort William and around Loch Ell and Loch Linnhe it

Lighthouse, Dunbar

happened in the modern way, with an interview on Radio Highland and a press handout from Ken Ross, the former telegraph boy, who now runs the service from his Inverness HQ.

There may yet be more routes to add to the current total. If the numbers of passengers have declined since the 1970s, it is largely because car ownership has exploded, not least in the Highlands. But there are ever increasing numbers of tourists and the buses are still a necessity in many rural areas for those who do not drive, or who simply enjoy the convenience and the friendliness of the wee red, much-loved buses.

Towards the autumn of that Silver Jubilee year, I took those quiet high and

Fishermen and Boy Steven deliver the scallop harvest into Kirkcudbright's bright and beautiful small harbour.

low roads north, south, east and west, following the postal cargoes on their journeys, sitting, watching, spying and for long Scots miles, eavesdropping lightly on the lives of the people, places and communities who use the service.

Beneath the smiling façade flits the ghost of another Scotland, one long since lost, remembered only in the old men's stories and melancholy heaps of stones with their echoes of extinguished lives. Pacing the pavane alongside is the industrial detritus of the past, now prettied up: mines which are now museums, lighthouses which no longer shine, mills which will never again grind, stations through which only memories whistle, schools where no child will ever stumble over the books and ABC. Gone to tourism or holiday homes nearly every one, awakened for the ersatz country life at weekends and for a few short summer weeks.

Old industries fled or dead. Village shops closed, no butcher, baker or anything-maker. And yet some things go on.

The fishing remains. Different catches perhaps for different markets –

scallops, crabs and all the crustaceans, fast frozen and faster flown to foreign tables. And sometimes even eaten at home, as are the fish from the farms, corralled, tamed and fiercely pink trout and salmon. People still shoot and stalk and cull and call it sport, thereby keeping the home tills turning in hotel, lodge and estate. The keepers and ghillies continue to patrol. Their dogs still bark and whine in the kennelling and the dull, flightless pheasant chicks scurry and peck around the yards unaware of the bright plumage and the fate which will come with their wings and that buried illusion of freedom.

Farming continues too, with tidy, golden, seemingly bountiful fields and healthy sheep grazing the hills. Despite set-aside and the EU's Common Agricultural Policy, some farmers survive in profit or in thrall to their bankers. EU subsidies are themselves subsidised with Bed & Breakfast, redundant fields are turned into nature trails and scrambles for mountain and motorbikes, and

Overleaf: KenRoss, Postbus controller, master of all he surveys.

Making hay while the sun shines high up near Leadhills in Lanarkshire.

visitors are made welcome and encouraged to ooh and aah at the new-born lambs tucked in beside the Aga. The old crops are being replaced by new harvests of tourists.

There are, however, also signs of new communities and new commercial enterprise hesitantly hatching. Hills are quarried to supply a motorway's foundations; fish and deer farms exploit what they can, while computer software firms, the new cottage industries, appear hard by the peat stacks of Granny's Hielan' hame.

I met people involved in most of these areas on or about the postbuses, never entirely sure as I sat and listened if I was tuning in to a rural rhapsody or requiem as they gossiped and chatted. Sometimes both themes played together in a discordant duet.

This, then, is a snapshot of that journey, a summer's soundbite. It is also, I hope, an appreciation of a service which remains almost uniquely that – a service. Run efficiently, certainly, and for profit, hopefully, but primarily fulfilling the needs of places and people too often forgotten. It is also an appreciation of all the drivers and their passengers who allowed me, briefly, to burrow into their lives and their remembrances, to ask how, where, why and when.

Neil Richerby and Konrad Daenhardt taking time off from making organs and making work for the Postbus which brings to their workshop door both orders and parts so that their customers can make music.

Evelyn Taylor and her unofficial co-driver, temporarily have time to stop and stare and enjoy the gentle East Lothian scenery.

CHAPTER TWO

OF SLOE GIN AND FAST DRIVERS

I began at the beginning, on that very first route, from Dunbar to Innerwick with Spott and its elongated scatter of houses in between. It is little more than twenty miles east of Edinburgh but down a bleak road with a bleaker sea at the end of it where the great cold bulk of Torness nuclear power station looms menacingly. It was another, crueller country, leeched of all colour. Shades of grey in a dark dawn, stretching into a greyer distance for miles and miles. Few people up yet and no warmth anywhere, except within the postbus. 'So, it's cold out', I said to the driver, Evelyn Taylor, to break the conversational ice as she decided whether she should or shouldn't zip the padded winter-weight sleeves into her jacket. It was after all late August. Evelyn discarded the sleeves, found a pair of fingerless gloves and agreed equably that yes it was generally cold in Dunbar at 7 a.m. In fact, she said, in her experience it was cold in most places at 7 a.m. Then she was away, with a grin in a puff of exhaled breath and a sea mist, to drop off the first letters of the day.

Post first, passengers later on Evelyn's run. We drove briefly down to those salt-dampened houses glaring out at the sludgy neighbouring sea, on to the old lighthouse without its light and the harbour with no ships and then up and away over the main road and into the country, to the farms and cottages, hours before Molly Lafferty will leave her home to join us.

On the way Evelyn and I warm together. She shows me the plum trees across the fields where she scrumps the ripe autumn Victorias and the house where her brother, the blacksmith, lives and works in the old way. We talk of other country matters, the decline in rural ways, and more happily of dogs and horses. Once in another life she trained horses for the showring and she says, casually throwing it away as she gears expertly down a hill, tigers too, in Germany.

'Useful trade,' I queried, 'for keeping the passengers in order?'

'Possibly,' she replied, 'possibly.'

I soon learned to be as unsurprised by tiger-training postbus drivers as I was by the cold on early mornings. But first I learned that this is not a job for conformists or the faint-hearted. The drivers acknowledge the fact with the disinterested patience that comes easily to men and women used to daily dealings with everything from raging ewes attempting grievous bodily harm to their tenderer parts, to enraged incomers who haven't yet learned (although they do, they do) to understand it is not always possible to deliver mail at 8 a.m. sharp.

There is, too, the famous rule book. The one which tells them what a driver may and may not do and which, in theory, is entirely sensible and indeed necessary. But in practice, behind the wheel of a postbus its stern admonitions and instructions can not always be followed to the absolute last letter.

Fares, it says, must be collected on boarding and passengers charged in accordance with the schedules of fares and conditions of service. Dead simple. No problem at all until your passengers are twenty-stone drunks who stagger into the bus and who fall comatose on its floor with nothing in their gaping pockets but an old button and a can of export. Try extracting a fare in accordance with the schedules from one of those. Or from foreigners who think postbuses come free, who smile and nod in every language but whose basic English lessons were not tuned to Scots voices and who, in the interests of international goodwill and the tourist trade, if not the conditions of service, cannot really be officiously or even officially tipped out at the top of some lonely glen.

And while dogs must never under any circumstances be allowed to occupy a seat, shifting an Alsatian long in tooth and short of temper off one isn't necessarily advisable. I know that because I tried. Once.

There is also the matter of the uniform. That it must be worn at all times is fair enough, but the previous strictures on such detail as when a top button may or may not be undone (not before the first of June and not after the last day in August, if you are more interested in the Rule than the drivers are) do today appear to have been a trifle petty. Like Evelyn's padded sleeves, there is

a proper time and season for everything. Including hats. They blame Postman Pat for the hats. Postman Pat, as most people aged between two and six can tell you, always wears his hat. He is never seen without his clamped on his cranium, while postbus drivers' heads are seldom seen with one.

But the uniform headgear does have one characteristic in its favour: it is apparently exactly the right size for landing a nice trout. Postbus drivers are prepared for anything.

Which is why Nigel Nice on the Broadford to Elgol route on Skye, driving in sight of a spectacular but dangerous, if more deceptively inviting, green, lucent sea than Evelyn's cold north-eastern water, wears climbing boots on his route. I don't think they are in the regulations either. Not that the boots are for leaping up the nearby Cuillins when the mood takes him, but to help bring down those who too frequently do, wearing only T-shirts, trainers and shorts.

Perhaps the government should erect signs in mountainous areas warning that strolling, walking or climbing there can seriously damage the health, not to mention the patience of those who have to extradite them from their mountain follies. Maybe a compulsory insurance scheme might concentrate the mind and increase walkers' equipment beyond that which is scarcely adequate for a saunter around an urban park. But there will always be those who cannot or will not grasp that the temperature, terrain and weather at the bottom of even the smallest peak are not ever repeated at the top, all those many feet above.

Nigel, originally from Chelmsford and already working for the Royal Mail, was on holiday in Applecross with his Scots wife when he saw his first postbus. 'That's for me,' he said and promptly applied. Twelve years on, there he is on the Elgol run, with three children, three cows, a clutch of hens, a couple of dogs, no TV but a violin, a piano preserved in the pantry, home-baked cakes on his kitchen table and no regrets at all about that mad initial impulse. He would even learn Gaelic if it wasn't for the grammar: 'Can't manage English grammar yet , can I?'

In the meantime his kids are speaking what they call 'the language' in school, while he's doing his bit by slowing down to Skye time, which makes the Spanish *mañana* seem something in much too much of a hurry. So Nigel has been building the steps down to his chaotic, cluttered home for

Gaelic is still a living and learning language in the school at Elgol - although the children, including his own, usually try to remember that Nigel Nice comes from Chelmsford and tease him in English.

24

approximately two years now. Every time he means to get down to it someone wants a hand with boatbuilding, to borrow of his mini-tractor or simply his time.

In Skye, it is just such behaviour, more than Gaelic grammar and tartan vowels, that brings a kind of belonging, an acceptance not always given to those who have been less careful of the niceties of the island ways than Nigel. His only regret is for the passing of a lifestyle, which even during his short years on the island he sees in retreat.

We stopped in a glen and he pointed out seven, eight houses once part of his route, now closed up, coloured snapshots in an estate agent's window, waiting for a buyer from beyond the island or, worse, decaying gently into death. Raw, new clearances which will soon moulder beside the still stones of those other, older but not forgotten evictions. Lost communities under grassy mounds, buried underground resentments.

But there can be some sort of a resurrection. Also on Nigel's route is Ian Anderson of supergroup Jethro Tull, whose Strathaird Estate flourishes. He is a new type of landlord from a new ruling class, the Lords of Rock, but who is still conscious of the old responsibilities, providing employment and thereby keeping the schools open and lifeblood flowing.

Mind you, Nigel, pulling sharply into the side, could do without the hazards of Anderson's fans, particularly those from Germany who have confused Skye's narrow roads for the Isle of Man's TT, and who would roar around and past and if they could, surely over Nigel's postbus in their black leathers, blue jeans and peaked hats instead of crash helmets. Worse are slowly loitering tourists doing ten miles an hour flat-out, with the camcorders hanging out the windows of their hatchbacks, eyes on them instead of their rear-view mirrors. Of course the views are absolutely fabulous, but in the meantime the doctor, ambulance, the hurrying native and postbuses need past sooner rather than later and at a tourist's pleasure. Besides, it is an offence to refuse to allow faster vehicles past on single-track roads. Indeed in that summer of 1993 a tourist was charged and fined for slow driving.

There are also the cyclists, either those who have ferried across their own machines or who have contributed to that new but now ubiquitous cottage industry, the bike-hire business, and who sometimes rhythmically, although more usually not, manage to straddle the middle of every island and most Highland roads.

Long miles , too, can be spent crawling behind caravans, often in convoy, three or four together, dawdling here, speeding up there, seemingly oblivious to cars and buses behind. Even when at rest caravans can escape popularity, especially in those shops, cafés and restaurants where their inhabitants ask for free water for the tea bags bought in some suburban supermart far away and take huge offence when it is refused. For caravans tend to travel heavy while contributing lightly to local economies.

Considering the number of miles travelled, postbus drivers have few battle scars – a bumper gone to a lorry here, a wing mirror lost to a tractor there. Although Nigel Nice did have £500 worth of damage following an altercation between his side door and a sheep, which the sheep won. Sheep are even more pervasive than caravans and on the whole less predictable, but the drivers are as aware of the beasts' woolly-headedness as any shepherd. They know where and when to expect them dawdling on their route, just as they know the timetables of the other country users who share their roads – the school buses,

The sheep at Glasnakille deciding against either suicide or a duel with the postbus. This time.

the agricultural reps and the milk tanker. They also know the seasons, when the combines roll, when the logging lorries lumber round, when the wheelie-bins, those Daleks of the dustbin trade, will loll and roll about the road, waiting for the rural rubbish run.

Postbus drivers listen assiduously to the weather forecasts, for the weather is foe as well as friend and can turn nasty very quickly indeed. Others forget at their peril. Bob Shaw can recall the day the Snowman's Rally came to his patch, through the woods between Forres and Braemoray. Bob knows how the weather in his area can flatter and deceive: pale sun will shine foolishly bright but not necessarily shift the black ice, while snow can be nowhere and suddenly it is everywhere. A bit like rallies, really, remarked Bob. For one minute the road is empty and the next it's a roar of mad motorists. As it was on that particular day, clear and crisp but with iced snow, hard-packed on the high road. Not at all like it had been down at the start of the stage in Forres. Bob parked at the bottom of a hill and watched as one by one the unwary spun into the ditches, skidded sideways and found themselves tossed like tonkas through the frosted trees. 'All of them. Of course the post was a wee bit late,' he says, ' but there was nothing I could do but sit and wait it out.' The breakdown and support vehicles came and went and then Bob eased himself and his Peugeot Estate into the appropriate gear and went safely on his way.

Drivers like Bob do not take chances with mail, passengers or themselves, although to those unused to country roads, this is perhaps not altogether obvious. Not least to the Swiss tourist I met, the one with the white knuckles, urgently seeking a lavatory at Achnasheen station on the West Highland Line who had driven down the steep Laide road with Murdo, the former French polisher from Glasgow, at the wheel.

'They should haf paper bags,' he suggested, through thin, green- tinged lips. 'Like they do on aeroplanes.'

Murdo smiled when I told him the story, amused but not at all put out, especially by tourists,

'And there was me thinking they had the odd wee hill in Switzerland too ,' he said.

Not only the roads and the routes but also the timetable, which ticks ever on, holds all drivers in thrall. It doesn't always accommodate the wood-cutting for the old lady who won't have her heat unless the postie obliges. And others told me more than once the tale, apocryphal no doubt, of the postie who saw a man collapse, dropped everything and ran for help. On the Monday, they say, he received his letter of commendation and on the Tuesday his official reprimand for abandoning his mail bag unattended on the pavement.

Postbus drivers become very proprietorial and indeed attached to their buses. They talk to them, and not only on Islay where every postbus has an official name. Instructions, Postal Mini Bus Drivers for the Attention of, exhorts them to sweep their buses daily, to tidy them and to give them a weekly wash and polish. For some drivers this is all much too casual and not nearly a sufficient enough toilet.

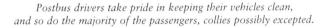

Postbus drivers take pride in keeping their vehicles clean,
and so do the majority of the passengers, collies possibly excepted.

*The Postbus comes to bleak Blackness Castle which once doubled as
Elsinore for Franco Zefferelli's film of Hamlet.*

Robin Laing in Linlithgow, off the M8, the main road between Edinburgh and Glasgow, would consider all this frightfully slipshod. Robin's bus is always immaculate, and if it wasn't expressly forbidden by the rules you could eat your breakfast, lunch and dinner off his bus' floor.

But then Robin, who came late to the job after many years of working in offices and for himself in something rather high- powered, is so polished, brushed and groomed that you could very likely eat your meals off him as well. His run is equally high- powered, with castles at both ends: The House of Binns – Scottish National Trust-owned but still called home by the family Dalyell, where peacocks squeal and preen on its lawns but which is presently shrouded in tarpaulin as a battle is waged as desperate as any fought by Black Tam Dalyell against the beetle and the rot – and Blackness, covered in history and scaffolding, where Zefferelli shot his *Hamlet*. And in between these twin castles are the smallholdings, larger farms and businesses, land and commerce side by side with smart new housing estates for those who work in the latter, and older, bigger, more gracious houses from which fast-commuting executives hurry into Edinburgh.

A route with wealth, (*nest page*) kinder than raw Dunbar, more domesticated even than Perthshire or Deeside, where nature has been tamed and corralled behind the motorway and knows its proper place. It suits Robin, who seems to know more about the des reses on his run than any estate agent, their value, acreage and possible selling price speculated over and assessed. But then Robin is, I suspect a new breed of driver. He has plans for his bus; he wants it full all day and very possibly all night. He may not be the fastest driver I met but he may well be the fittest – he runs the walking parts of his route, does Robin, and all before a bite of breakfast, in his full regulation uniform and tie and without breaking sweat either.

Postbus Driver Sandy Shairp who remains tolerant of all his customers, even the tourists, school children and dogs.

Sandy Shairp, from Luing, that little island slung out on the edge of the Atlantic between Oban and Jura is of an older, not to say slower tradition. But when the Royal Mail took his Sherpa up to Glasgow for their twenty-fifth anniversary party, his reunion with it outside the Post Office in Cullipool was like a shepherd finding a long-lost collie. He patted it. He walked around it. He felt it all over. He made sure the heathens had returned it in a fit and

Overleaf: Linlithgow and its Palace in the gloaming, dreaming of old ghosts and older glories, where Mary, Queen of Scots slept and Stuart kings hunted.

Lochindorb, where the Wolf of Badenoch once had his Island Lair but which is stalked by less warlike men these days like driver George Macintosh whose only weapon is his accordion.

healthy state. For the sentimental it was, I suggested, a sight to bring tears to the eyes and dissolve the hardest of hearts.

'Rural buses,' he explained not a bit abashed or embarrassed, 'should not be treated like town vehicles.' Much the same, said Sandy, echoing Nigel and Evelyn, as rural and urban life.

In the main the postbus drivers' windscreens are not rose-tinted. They respect the countryside and the majority will tell you, without prompting, that they never tire of the infinite variety of it and of its inhabitants, animal and human. They appreciate the beauty which is part of their everyday lives. But they also have a clear-eyed view of it from their buses. Not least because so many of their regular passengers are the old and the poor who cannot afford cars and who, even if they wanted to, do not have the option of moving to warmer, kinder climes when the winter winds blow cold and expensively.

One morning early into my odyssey, on George McIntosh's Grantown-on-Spey run, we had passed in and out of the dead village of Dava which he could remember when it was a place to which people were proud to belong and who cherished its independence from other, bigger places. Now little is left except disconnected houses and disconnected lives. A sad, lost hamlet made sadder because it is but one of many such displaced communities. We got out while George pointed to this and that. The school here, the library in that building there, and we walked along the road which used to lead to the station and the dance-hall. Both gone too. One to renovation as a private house, the other to ruin. George says, more in anger than sorrow, that when Beeching cut the railway, he cut the heart out of Dava and stopped its life dead.

But later, looking at the Lochindorb that afternoon with nothing on it but the ripple from a man, his line and his boat, he sought and found a sort of consolation.

'This remains,' he said sweeping his arms around. 'This will never go or be taken from us.'

Much has been taken already and people worry that what remains may also disappear. So men like George use the countryside and its free harvests while they can. They continue to cut peats, to fish and roam the hills: there is still sport and free booty to be had without a laird or his lackey claiming it for their own.

Which was how I learned to make sloe gin. Steuart Murray, who drives out of Kirkcudbright down in Scotland's southern bump, is the expert although his customer and friend Sandy Sproat disputes it. We sat in Sandy's kitchen one bright morning, with its collection of Arts and Craft pottery casually displayed – Kirkcudbright is and always has been artier and craftier than most – while they discussed the best mix of sloes and sugar and gin. Once Sandy and Steuart and the teapot were through and it was time to take the children to school, we went on our way, delivering the mail (and the children) before getting on with the real business of the day, searching out the berries for the beet-red brew. I have a pint of it in front of me, a happy memory trapped in alcohol.

Sandy Sproat and his wife who always have time to stop for a cup of tea - frequently out of one of their enviable collection of local arts and crafts pottery - with the postbus driver.

33

With all his passengers and post safely delivered, George Macintosh relaxes with his accordion which always speaks his language.

CHAPTER THREE

WHITE SETTLERS AND GREEN TREES

All that long summer I heard expressed many opinions about a tribe known the length and breadth of the country as the White Settlers, those incomers who have moved in increasing numbers into Scotland's rural communities. There had always seemed a large measure of affection in the universal sobriquet and a certain tolerance too. But there is something of the confessional about the wee red buses. Perhaps it is the shape of the Sherpas and Land Rovers or maybe the enclosed space and metal grille between driver and public, because an awful lot of omissions and commissions are admitted to within its confines. In soft Highland tones, in quiet island lilts and in the rougher, broader accents of the Borders and Scotland's north-east, I was given an insight into an uneasy interdependence.

Some people were slightly ashamed of articulating what sounded like prejudice, conscious that it wasn't altogether right; but on the bus, secure amongst their own, they felt free to discuss their irritations about the way in which those from outwith an area would move in, as they saw it, almost

Jack and Jenny Kubale, Strathard Guest House Elgol

colonise it and submerge an old culture beneath something alien, new and not altogether welcome.

So they would recount the latest tales of what they considered to be the incomers' insensitivity. Of, for instance, the Rotary Club, committeed by outsiders, who were building a bonfire, buying fireworks and fuelling up their portable barbecues for Guy Fawkes, waiting for the plaudits and the applause from the grateful locals. And not understanding at all that by remembering the 5th of November they were also busy forgetting the 31st of October, Hallowe'en and yet another Scottish tradition had gone the way of so many others. Indeed a very small thing, but our own and to some people something that mattered.

Or so they said on the bus. Of course much of it was general grumble, a safe moan to be enjoyed and frequently too a quiet laugh at those who did not understand the ways of their new-found land. So the English couple in Aberfeldy who had had the new garden shipped in from the expensive landscapers in the south, lock, stock and lupin – but without a rabbit or (more particularly) a deer-proof fence – and who lost every last root of it over a single night, was good for a smile and the lightening of an otherwise dreary journey on the bus. The old man who told the story did so with more amusement than malice. And while the couple will not know of that morning's brief merriment they will remember the cuttings and plants that same old man brought quickly to their door – along with advice on fencing.

There were certainly other, larger issues. Not least housing. Tales on the bus of sons and daughters unable to buy homes in the places in which they were born because they can't afford to compete financially with the deeper pockets and larger purses of the new good-lifers. There is a crisis in rural housing, acknowledged and recognised by Shelter and local authorities. Unemployment, the lack of council houses and the generally smaller salaries in country communities have all combined to price-out many locals. At one level this is accepted, just as they accept that many of the houses now occupied by the incomers had been ruins, rejected and neglected by locals. But sometimes it is easier to blame the stranger from without than the folk next door.

In the 1980s there was, without doubt, a feeding frenzy on Scottish rural real estate. People sold in the over-priced and over-hyped housing market in the south-east of England and reinvested and relocated in Scotland. The Sunday supplements were not complete without the ritual story of the couple who had exchanged a semi in Croydon for a castle in Caithness. Others suffered from the Basil syndrome and thought they could make a Gleneagles out of every surplus manse or abandoned mansion and inevitably ended up with McFawlty Towers. Rather less publicised is the number who have, in the 1990s, been forced to sell up as they found out the hard way that keeping the home fires burning hotly in the north of Scotland is considerably more expensive than in the warmer south. And that playing Mine Host both successfully and profitably is not , after all a role for an amateur, no matter how enthusiastic.

One hotel near Dornoch has had six English owners in as many years. Every postbus driver had a similar tale to tell. The converted lodge with the fast-fading designer curtains at every window, ragged and dragged paintwork out of *Country Living* on the walls but only two guests to sit down to the gourmet grub and the roaring fire. Soon the carefully contrived menu is obscured by the desperate handwritten sign advertising B & B, bar snacks and coach parties welcome. Meanwhile the post is dropping off bills by the bundle.

More influential are the absentee landlords who buy and sell estates with little apparent thought for the people who live and work on them. The real toffs have all gone. Now the laird is as likely as not to be a pension fund or insurance company. Or bankrupt. Down in Grantown-on-Spey, on George McIntosh's route, is Castle Grant which, even if it still seems to stand high and proud among its policies and woodlands, has lost its soul. It is empty, near derelict, a peeling whitewashed ruin, on the market that summer of '93, waiting for a new owner to turn it into something, anything which could pay for the upkeep of the place. The farm is still worked but everything else is rotting and gone. The orchards, the outhouses, the stables, the gardens whose care and cultivation in the old days sustained its own community of servants. Now only the swallows keep busy, flying in and out of the abandoned barns, swinging from rotten eaves, building their nests where once humans made theirs.

George regrets the passing of that grander age when the family at the castle had their own private railway halt, disguised in an exuberant, mock-turreted folly. But noblesse obliged, at least in George's remembrances of those days long past: 'You see, we respected them, gave them their place. And in return they looked after us. They kept everything going.'

Some of them still do. There is Balmoral itself, of course, and also the Queen's neighbours, the Farquharsons of Invercauld who live in Braemar Castle.

When the postbus and Stuart MacLeod-Slater dropped me off, to search for cashmere in the woollen shops, to wander through the ferociously restored souvenir and tourist centre and to admire Braemar's park where they hold the Highland Games and for which the royal family wear the obligatory tartan, the locals, the majority without local accents, continually pointed out to me that Braemar is a real castle, not some Victorian pastiche.

But better that than the neighbouring Mar Lodge estate, bought by one of America's richest men, John Kluge, for his wife Pamela, the former beauty

Invercauld

38

queen who yearned, again according to the gossip, to be but a caber throw
away from a real Queen. The big house, with its herds of antlers and pop-
eyed deer heads mounted on every wall, was restored and made ready for the
new owner. But alas, before the new bathrooms and the Jacuzzi could gush or
Mrs Kluge welcome HM for tea and toasted scones in the baronial hall, there
was first a fire which destroyed much of the refurbishment. Then the marriage
itself was over and now the lodge and all its acres and livelihoods they
supported are for sale again at a hugely inflated price. Prince Charles would
like it to be bought for the nation but more likely it will soon be just another
holiday home. On the grand scale certainly but no different really from all
those other holiday homes, another irritant. For the holiday-homers stand
accused above all others of not only out-bidding the locals but of changing
living houses into petrified palaces with every mod con in place except the one
that counts – a permanent presence. So there are no children for the schools,
no customers for shop or Post Office and another community becomes
nothing but a country dormitory where the townies go for rest and
recuperation. Where letters, never mind the postbus, come rarely.

   Almost as unpopular are the commuters who leave early and return late and whose names are known to the postman but whose faces are never seen and whose country lives last for little more than a long weekend. In their wake appear developments which do not always fit sympathetically into their setting: the Tudorbethan kit house overlooking a border loch and all those twee tarted-up cottages with un-Scottish names, coach lamps at their doors and wagon wheels marking their garages. I did begin to search for the scapegoat, someone, anyone to blame for turning wild and beautiful places into just another tamed suburb.

It is, of course, a mistake to assume that all such follies belong and are inhabited entirely by those born firth of Scotland. Those bungalows and ranch houses are as likely – and sometimes more likely – to be occupied by a doctor from Glasgow as a retired London banker. In fact some of the least aesthetically appealing houses I saw are built by locals or those returning to their Highland and Island roots. Usually those of a certain age. There are many, maybe too many, areas in Scotland's prettier byways, in the lowlands as well as the Highlands, which can look like one vast retirement home with an average age of seventy-something .

I drove into Bowden Cross near Melrose with young, piratical Neil Hall at the wheel, his single earring glinting as the sun moved high in the early afternoon sky. Nothing else stirred apart from the perfume from the flowers in all the empty gardens behind high privet hedges. I found myself whispering, as if in a graveyard. It was lovely, I said but deathly if not deadly.

'This,' Neil whispered back, 'is as lively as Bowden Cross gets.' We left, the bus's diesel and a single barking dog rude intrusions into this, one of heaven's petrified waiting rooms.

Young voices come as a relief, no matter their origin. On Luing where the postbus takes the children to school, many of them speak with tongues tutored far from the island but here the alien voices are welcome. For slowly the small deserted townships of houses built for the slate quarries, which closed some twenty years ago, are being sold and reoccupied. And Sandy Shairp and the other long-time residents aren't asking any of these newcomers from whence they came, grateful only that they guarantee the island the hope of a future instead of old memories.

Anyway, he says, equally, 'They soon slow down to our pace of things . . . there's nothing like a bit of damp, I always say to slow a person down.'

There is indeed plenty of damp on Luing, along with its own particular breed of shaggy cattle and the relicts of its industrial past, still visible in the slate slides which slither down the slopes to rest on the shore, petrified monuments to the near past when the quarries gave work and some small wealth to the island.

Luing, with the ferry (crewed by an Englishman) heaving backwards and forwards across the narrow Atlantic strip of sea between it and Easdale, seems more at ease with itself than many places and all the other islands I saw.

School children at Luing.

It is not a particularly pretty place, mostly flat and windblown. No lairds at the big house, indeed no big houses at all. Nothing tarted up for visitors although they still trickle through in the summer. Sandy pointed out the old mill which was just that, an old mill, falling to bits, not restored in any way as it would probably have been elsewhere. I think I liked that, if only because so many roads lead to places which didn't seem quite real, which looked as if they existed only for tourists and their trade. In the winter, Luing must be bleak and cold as well as damp but, like its mill, it has not been made into something it is not.

It has also largely resisted that other Scottish invader whose conquest of the land has been much more complete than that of any other. The fiscus fir does not intrude into every view, glen and every hill as it does elsewhere. Surely this is the most intrusive incomer of them all. A triffid army which has taken over, obliterating everything else, changing the ecology and the landscape on its awesome yet terrible march over Scotland. From the Borders northwards their ranks are never long from sight. Nothing seems to live within the spread of their dark battalions where the sun cannot penetrate. They overpower the roads, darken the light and rearrange every view. The hills are buried in them and lost, despite the walkways carved through them

41

Cullipool

by the Forestry Commission as some inadequate sop for all that the trees have stolen.

Up in Royal Deeside it is still possible to see how it could all have been so different. Stuart MacLeod-Slater drove me into the remains of the old Caledonian forest, preserved at least in part by Queen Victoria's vision, where the trees sit lightly, sharing the space, allowing the sun in as well as all that eternal shade. And where moss and ferns and flowers flourish too. For these trees are proper trees which know the seasons, which lose their leaves, and which most of all remind us of what a forest should be. A mixture of deciduous, hard wood, soft wood and evergreens, with no one single species dominating. As it should be everywhere. There is hope that future forestry will be nearer the old. There is no denying that the trees are essential to the economy and provide employment.

It would be simplistic and indeed wrong to blame the incomers for every ill. But fear of change and of the future drives people into uncomfortable places and unthinking nationalisms. The old histories and hurts die hard, with the clearances still remembered in story and song and everywhere visible stones which were once homes for those families driven off for sheep. There are other memories too. At the head of Loch Rannoch are the barracks built for the Redcoats, to crush the rebellious Scots. The postbuses still travel the roads and routes first mapped out and tramped over by General Wade and his army of occupation. It is less romantic to remember that many were driven out by their own countrymen, and that it was not only the English who accepted a Hanoverian King's shilling.

Like many walkers and hikers on the Rannoch Moor, the postbus and its passengers usually find time to stop and admire the river tumbling through the Bridge of Gaur.

*Opposi
Linn of D*

One of Islay's distilleries at Bowmore where the great copper stills turn peat water and barley into liquid magic which has made the island famous wherever men - and women - lift a glass of malt whisky. And the postbus stops by some of their doors.

Post Office at Port Charlotte.

CHAPTER FOUR

TOUJOURS AUCHAYE THE NOO

Cameron McGhie is the perfect island gentleman, good humoured and droll, a postbus Para Handy if ever there was one, who drives back and forward between Port Ellen and Portnahaven. He stopped outside the Bruichladdich Distillery and returned after the usual courtesies with a bottle of its famous malt. Not for himself, of course, but for a passenger who wanted a sample of one of Islay's better-known liquid souvenirs. Cameron naturally wouldn't hear of allowing them to trudge around a dreich Port Charlotte, not when Bruichladdich's copper stills were there on his route. 'No, no,' he insisted. It was absolutely out of the question, no doubt about it at all. Island hospitality and all that that implies.

Meanwhile there were other, more serious obligations that day for Cameron: death notices to be carried and put into every Post Office ('For Money Orders, Savings Bank, Parcel Post, Telegraph, Insurance and Annuity Business', as it said on the enamelled plaques in curly 1930s script outside each one) on the road to Portnahaven. He put them in the window, beside all the posters advertising aerobic classes – aerobics these days in Islay seem to be outnumbering Gaelic classes by three to one – and outings for the over-sixty-fives. The stiff white cards, heavily black-bordered, respectfully requesting mourners to attend the funeral service in Bowmore Round Church. Round, Cameron explained, so that the Devil and his servant, Sin, were denied a corner in which to hide.

The funeral was that of a local farmer. The fact that the whole island was invited to attend was not unusual, for death is still a social as well as a sad business in the Hebrides. What was perhaps more unusual, even Cameron agreed, was the deceased's request that he should be interred six feet down into his own land, on the side of a green hill overlooking a greener sea, instead of over the wall, inside the plain Bowmore kirkyard. For all that it would still be a good Christian burial, for Islay is nothing if not a good Christian island, even if it does fragment itself between the Lord's many different mansions on earth. But they are definitely good, God-fearing folk who will do anything for their neighbours, who make visitors truly welcome, who will always, with and without a postbus, go that extra mile or a few yards up a distillery path. Travelling the flat Islay roads on a cold morning, past the little towns, over the peat bogs, almost always with the smell, sound and sight of the sea, carrying people, post and gossip, is as warming as a dram of Bruichladdich itself.

And then into Portnahaven itself, journey's end, a tidy, whitewashed, steep-streeted village climbing up and down and around the bay where the seals surface to sing and bask in the sunshine. Lovely to hear, Cameron said, something not to be missed. Portnahaven is also where Cameron parks every morning outside the public lavatories in front of the single stark terrace of council houses which look as if they have been picked up complete, a job-lot from some 1960s city overspill. And where, once the postbus has delivered the mail and the papers, boxes of wedding cake and three tennis racquets (although I saw no tennis court in Portnahaven) to Mrs Cooper in her Post Office and dropped off a grandchild at his gran's, Cameron eats his lunch and reads the morning paper.

It is the perfect time for any passengers making the trip both ways to walk down the steep brae to attend the seal concerto. Unfortunately, on the day I was there the sunshine was otherwise engaged and the seals had gone wherever sensible seals go on days when the rain comes down and the wind gets up. It was early September, the sort of day on which Evelyn Taylor in Dunbar would have zipped-in her padded sleeves. Cameron's bus was, after the journey, nicely heated up. *I* was not and neither, it seemed, was Portnahaven. 'Is there,' I asked Cameron as the chill gathered around me, 'a cafe?'

But of course, he replied, and indeed had he not himself pointed it out on the way in? That cottage which the builders were even now working away on and which would be opening in, oh, no more than two weeks. Just in time to miss the tourist trade, I said, but Cameron just smiled the Islay smile.

The postbus climbs up Portnahaven's empty streets and braes to Mrs Cooper, the postmistress.

The door shut on the warmth, Cameron, his paper and well-deserved break. Outside the wind blew, a window banged repeatedly and a dog limped past and howled when it saw me. All Portnahaven needs on a bleak day, I thought, was John Wayne riding into town. Or possibly Alfred Hitchcock. When Cameron had had his lunch, an hour later, and I had perambulated around Portnahaven's attractions in my summer skirt and shoes and seen no one, nothing but the flicker, at 11.30 a.m. of TV screens behind curtains in those neat, closed-in little streets and where even the cocks do not seem to dare to crow before noon, Cameron asked why I had not gone to the pub.

I had seen no pub, I said. Cameron thought for a long minute.

'Ah well,' he explained, 'Maureen doesn't have a sign up. Because she's not for letting everyone know it's a pub, you understand.'

47

As we swung up and away from the village I saw people begin to emerge from their houses, almost hesitantly, in one and twos, converging on the Post Office as if our departure had released them from an enchantment and they had been kissed awake by the postbus. There was quite a crowd of them by the time we had accelerated past the church at the top, the one with twin doors which jointly serves both Portnahaven and Port Wemyss. Two neighbouring villages so close that it is impossible to say where one begins and the other ends but whose devout churchgoers refuse to go through the same portal to worship the same God, sing the same hymns, listen to the same sermon, before the same pulpit and same minister. No one seemed to think any of this in any way strange; indeed I expect it was as normal as Portnahaven's pub with no sign.

Islay seems very different, the only place where they give their postbuses proper names and name plates – Red Roddie, Minnie Bus and Scarlet – although this is an innovation from the local manager, James Stewart, an incomer originally from Larkhall in Lanarkshire, who organised the naming competition for local schoolchildren to celebrate the postbus's twenty-fifth anniversary. With Postman Pat models as prizes it was a great success and, suitably encouraged, James decided to run another quiz for adults. He printed leaflets, organised advertising and publicity then waited for the completed entries to flow in; he waited some more and those few which did finally arrive completed were invariably postmarked Croydon or Glasgow or Cardiff but not Islay.

Unfortunately, James, efficient and energetic but slightly bewildered by his island postal fiefdom, had forgotten to take into account Islay time which, like Skye's, runs some beats behind the mainland's. His own wife met the proof of it head-on in Bowmore her first week on the island when she asked a local the time and was told with infinite courtesy, 'October.' James should have realised, too, he says now, that Islay time doesn't allow space for a quiz, which was won, naturally, by a holidaymaker. Other duties take up his time, among them spending an afternoon down on the shore scooping up some of Islay's fabled silver sand to send to a wealthy American who requested a boxful to turn into a vase. The gentleman also sent a blank cheque which says something about the perception abroad of Royal Mail – and Islay – honesty.

Americans and their wishes are sometimes easier to fathom than customers closer to home, although he is not quite so sure about the occasion on which another American mistook him for her porter. It was on a day the afternoon plane, universally and possibly affectionately known as the Paraffin Budgie by those who fly on it and which bears a remarkable resemblance to a postbus with wings attached, was late even by Islay time. Cameron and the other drivers' shifts were long over but the Royal Mail cannot be left so James himself drove down to the airport where he found, standing alone, a little old lady who was as distressed as only little old ladies can be when they are in a

The anniversary plaques on the Islay postbuses, where, of course, they do most things differently including these official names for the postbus, chosen by the Island's schoolchildren.

foreign country, their accommodation is miles away and there is no sign of any suitable transport .

There was only James and the postbus. Gallantly, although her hotel was well out of his way, James did his bit for the Post Office image and island hospitality and offered his services. The lady's distress vanished. She climbed into the bus. Then, when she was sitting comfortably, she snapped her fingers. 'Driver,' she ordered, 'get my bags.' And James did. He counted all forty of them in, and at the hotel he counted them all out again and then carried every last vanity case and wardrobe trunk up to her room. As he left, she pressed all of 50p into his hand.

Postbus driver, Liz Stewart, an incomer from Glasgow who has few problems with either islanders or passengers but plenty with the deer and sheep who are determined to commit hari kiri under Minnie Bus's wheels.

Liz Stewart drives another of the buses, from Bowmore to Port Askaig where the ferry crosses the choppy mile to Jura and where Strathclyde Region maintains a wholly deserted but extremely fine set of pristine public lavatories, all stainless steel and soft recessed lighting. As someone said, the Region does not always seem to know what to do with its far-off island outlands, so when in doubt they build yet more public lavatories.

'I think it's because they don't believe we have indoor sanitation,' a man said to me in Port Charlotte, 'and that we use our baths to keep peat in.' He ruminated for a long minute, then added: 'Of course some folk do indeed, for can you not get a lot of peat in a bath now.'

And he looked at me gravely from out of those blue island eyes until I played the game too and laughed.

Liz is also an incomer, originally from Glasgow, who moved to the island with her parents when she was a young teenager and although she soon returned to the city to train as a nurse she gave up her career to marry an islander. They now have three children born and schooled in Islay, but Liz acknowledges without the slightest hint of either resentment or surprise that she will never be fully accepted: 'Of course my children will be, although not until I am safely dead.'

50

The islanders have seen much of their way of life disappear. Those unwelcome apocalyptic horsemen of the twentieth century have not passed them by: unemployment, alcoholism, emigration and immigration – all have ridden through these precarious, self-contained but not necessarily self-supporting communities. They are conscious of their reputation as modern remittance men, reliant on the dubious bounty of the DSS and of sons and daughters who have gone, voluntarily or otherwise, to seek success beyond the island.

That story is told by the mail itself, not only in all those dole cheques but in too many letters and cards stamped from faraway places. And no matter how warm the welcome to incomers, occasional or more permanent, there is a reserve and a holding back behind all those gentle words, soft accents and good humour. They are a people seen through a glass darkly, hiding behind a mask of good manners, consciously clothing themselves in a carapace of Caledonian cuteness. Toujours Auchaye the Noo. But who exactly is laughing at whom? That, too, is not always entirely obvious. On Islay was it me with my notebook, picking up my quaint anecdotes, or Cameron, amusing himself watching the slicked city lady in her unsuitable shoes and clothes, coping with Portnahaven?

On Skye, Nigel Nice's run passes the house of the late Lilian Beckwith

51

who made a modest fortune and not a few enemies with her simplistic, obvious satires on Highland life. But, I wondered, re-reading the books after my own journey's end, who was in the end most revealed, in the spaces between the lines? Not necessarily the islanders, who slipped easily into their droll roles but who in the end gave up very little of their real selves.

Barra has retained its identity more than most places, not unconnected with the fact that Gaelic is spoken every day by approximately ninety percent of the population, and has that same sense of something veiled, beyond the ken of those whose ancestors do not lie in the Barra burial grounds.

Yet, on a day out with Niall MacPherson, who drives the bus from the Traigh Mhor airstrip on Barra's beach to Bagh A Tuath (Northbay) and who until the 1970s did his travelling on slightly larger transport than mini-buses when he was in the Merchant Navy, there is much that is beguiling in Barra. For instance, for a townie like me, who hardly knows her own neighbours' names, finding herself greeted and welcomed by every person met, however casually, on the roads or in the shops it is a refreshing novelty. People never pass by on the other side, figuratively or otherwise.

Contradictions abound on the island. The beauty of Barra is not any cosy, postcard prettiness, tamed by farmers or altered for the convenience of foresters. Barra, with its small crofts, common grazings, peat bogs, few roads, wildness and lonely, high places where only the birds visit, has in many visitors' eyes a natural, uncontrived beauty, cut off from the mainland by the sea and bordered by hidden beaches unwalked by all but the most determined of wanderers. Certainly those who live in Barra are proud of its uncompromised charm, which makes it all the more surprising that almost every house and croft, even the newest, is garnished with rubbish. Nothing is put away, everything is left to rot – a wheelbarrow here, agricultural artefacts mouldering over there beside the car which turned up its tyres a generation before. The beaches are also littered. Some, perhaps the majority, brought in by the tides from the ships which use the seas as a marine trash-can. But it cannot be denied that some of it is home grown. Yet beside every house stands a bin, bearing on its side the words, 'Na Cuir Luath Theth An', which Niall translated for me: 'No hot ashes to be put in bin'. Nor much of anything else as far as I could see.

Along the road from the airport, where the plane lands on a runway which is part of the shingled shore and where the tides and sea decide the timetable instead of man, Niall turns seamlessly from friendly postman into informed, unpaid guide, a Tourist Board dream, pointing out all the landmarks with insight and humour, knowing everything and everyone. On our left, the largest natural fish farm known to man; on the right, Compton Mackenzie's old home which is now used as a base for extracting the shells from the beach which are then used as the harl which coats so many of the newer houses on

The runway, the beach, the paraffin budgie and Barra.

Barra, making them gleam and glisten when touched by the sun. The bus and its passengers gaze and gasp at the wonder of it all. Cockles galore but few trees. They are scarce on the island and those that do grow are usually stunted, Hebridean bonsai, cultured by poor soil and unremitting winds straight from the Atlantic.

There are also very few gardens although there is one glorious exception, a little Eden, bright with flowers and where trees in their hundreds are being coaxed and encouraged to grow. It is Niall's own. For in the years since he returned to Barra and the family croft, where he built his home with the conservatory in the front and where the Minch swells at the back, he has laboured to grow an English country garden in this most Scottish of islands.

Niall McPherson.

He is not surprised or dismayed that others do not make the attempt. As he says, when you are grubbing out a living with a few sheep and a cow, tending roses is not high on the priority list. But, without criticising his neighbours, he does wonder aloud if the dole, necessary as it undoubtedly is, has not taken some of the initiative from the islanders. Although perhaps that might be changing as small enterprises, like his trees and the Co-op, strive for growth. Meanwhile, those of us with our easy lives on the mainland should perhaps give pause to think of these people, scrabbling in the freezing tides on their hands and knees for a poor pailful of cockles.

Niall, contemplating his garden and driving the postbus, says it is a good life all-round on Barra for a man who has been and seen everywhere, who has quartered the world and who has chosen to come home again. He has seen changes. Of the old black houses with their rough, sloping walls, rougher thatches and grudging windows, there is little left but stones. Occasionally one is retained as a byre or storehouse, and even more rarely are they restored and made habitable and suitable for modern living. Most islanders buy the kit houses which may not be my ideal Granny's Hielan' Hame but which, for those who have to live on Barra all year round, where dusk lasts twenty-four long hours in December, are not only snug and warm but much more easily maintained than those authentic, traditional crofts.

But traditional customs still linger on. Niall knows that few doors on his

Everything in Barra is Gaelically correct, including the Post Office and the Royal Mail.

route will ever be locked.

'Ach we only used to do that at the Glasgow Fair,' he says. 'But they don't come down now any more, they go to Spain. Which is, in my opinion, not a bad thing at all.'

Even if the door is for some unexplained reason closed against him and the post, a neighbour will always accept a parcel. He also knows when someone is away. You cannot change your shirt, they say, in a place like Barra without everyone knowing, which may not allow privacy but nevertheless guards against any OAP lying undiscovered on her floor for days and weeks.

There is also the Gaelic. Every street and signpost is now written in the first language of the people. The common tongue on Niall's run is Gaelic which, versatile and poetic as it is, cannot always suit every postal occasion, including recorded deliveries. Block letters in Gaelic is block letters. And, of course, the language has other uses and provides yet another, less easily breached barrier against strangers. As I drove round with Niall, at each stop on our way he would point back at me on the rear seat and say a few words. The islanders nearly always laughed and when I asked Niall to translate, he said was he not after telling them all what a fine person I was indeed.

But later, as the plane lifted me up into the sky again and back to Glasgow and postbuses new, I wondered, in Barra, in Gaeldom, in the islands with these complex people, how could I be sure of that or indeed of anything very much at all?

All washed up at Cove.

CHAPTER FIVE

KAMIKAZE COLLIES
AND OTHER ANIMALS

There are many wild animals lurking out there in postbus country. Mink, those vicious escapees from their farms who decimate the hen runs, rabbits immune to myxomatosis, methodical and destructive, four-legged furry locusts munching on everything in their path; and then there was also me at 6 a.m. on the high road to Laide, breakfasting on very stale cake and warm Coke. The hotel in which I had savoured the ersatz chips and reconstituted fish the previous evening kept, it seemed, rather later morning hours than me. Or the Royal Mail. So, they said, it would be quite impossible to provide me with anything to eat before 8 a.m.

'That's when the dining room opens, you see, love.'

I asked for a kettle for my room instead. Sadly, however, I was not sufficiently loved to be given one even when I promised to provide my own tea bags because as mine hostess said: 'Sorry, but we never do that because people steal kettles, don't they, love?'

I wasn't people, I said, I was me and although I wasn't actually carrying

references from other hoteliers to prove it, I had never stolen a kettle in my life. She considered this for a minute.

'Ah well, yes, but if we give you one, everyone will want one, won't they, love?'

I was the only person in residence.

Which might explain why they were so reluctant to let me leave. Unfed, unwatered and definitely unkettled at 5.30 a.m., I found every window and the front door double-locked, with no safe way out except through a bolted back kitchen. The burglar alarm, I gladly report, was much more efficient than the service and also extremely loud. Sorry, love.

So there I was in my lay-by with the day-old cake and Coke, when I realised that I was not quite alone in my reverie. There was a vixen with two half-grown cubs nosing the air on the other side of the road before crossing on her own, then lifting her sharp muzzle and harsh-calling the cubs to join her, and when they didn't immediately respond, returning to the other side and nip, nipping at their bony flanks. Three times she took them backwards and forwards, teaching them some red fox road code, keeping them always on the move, quickly marking the spot each time she crossed, until the wind stirred and she caught the whiff of me and they were off, jumping down the tangled slope towards the sea and away, tails high, russet wraiths in the pallid early sun. I drove on to Laide, feeling better.

The wildest animals by far, however, are not foxes: they are cloaked in that most cunning of camouflages – domesticity and obedience – for they are the kamikaze collies.

Dogs, *all* dogs, are, as everybody in the Royal Mail knows, the principal hazard of the postie's life. On the noticeboard in every delivery office are posters warning against canine attack and telling those who are bitten the correct, formal procedure, although the majority prefer something more informal, if possible a large-sized boot. Although it is said that demon letterboxes, especially when cunningly sited by aesthetically-minded architects three inches from the bottom of a door, run the mutts a close second. But in

general dogs inflict more damage on the mail and its deliverers and shred more letters and tear more fingers and flesh. All drivers have their story to tell and scars to show, not least of owners who seem to believe that it is their dog's God-given right to chew postmen. Only Sandy Shairp in Luing seemed immune.

'Ach,' he said when I enquired about the dogs on his route, 'they all just wag at me, don't they now?'

And so they do but then everyone and everything, I should think, wags at Sandy, myself included. There is something about the man which leaves most people feeling smiling and happy.

Evelyn Taylor at Dunbar is minus some muscle and tissue high up on her shoulder into which an Australian Ridgeback once fixed his fangs, inflicting in an instant more harm than ever the tigers managed. Evelyn likes dogs but not their teeth, so now there's one animal fewer on her route, formally dispatched by the vet's hypodermic after due judicial and postal review.

But the mutt which put Allan Gallacher's trousers in intensive care in Dunoon still lives to bite another day. It was, said Allan, all his own fault, as he drove me up by the Holy Loch, round the back of the sugar almond-coloured houses which used to house the American sailors from the old Polaris base. Allan is as philosophical about their departure as he is about the seriously damaged trousers.

George McIntosh loups lightly over a gate even although there is not a dog in sight.

'See, he's been after me for years, that one. Clever with it. Hides from me,' he recounted. 'So I didn't spot him, did I, until too late and there was him with his teeth and there was me louping over the fence, taking the emergency exit out.'

Sadly Allan misjudged his jump and left largish lumps of his trousers behind. He bore the dog no ill will.

'I mean, fair's fair. It wasn't him got me really but the fence.'

In Barra, Niall MacPherson, ever resourceful and thoughtful, has an ingenious solution to the problem. Niall, who knows the best way to do most things – including sending me, in my peerie heels, to deliver the post up the steepest paths on his route: 'It'll stop you getting all stiff,' he said considerately – visits any new pups on his route a soon as they're weaned.

'I make a great fuss of them, you see and then, well, even if they attack my colleagues, they don't attack me at all.'

However should Niall co-opt you as temporary postie (unpaid) I have a small word of warning about Barra dogs. Unlike their owners they are not, on the whole, bilingual but like the unpronounceable signposts and dustbins, stubborn Gaelic monoglots, which I discovered the sharp way up Niall's steep paths. When Messrs Baedeker get around to producing, as they surely will, a

60

phrase book for Barra and other islands where the language is spoken, perhaps they should consider including the Gaelic for 'good doggie' in it.

These dogs are ordinary dogs, doing ordinary dog-like things and causing ordinary dog-like damage. They are an entirely different breed from the kamikaze collies, the wildest beasts of them all, to whom postbus drivers, their trousers, their flesh and the post itself – are incidental objectives, minor obstacles to be overcome on the way to the real war. Kamikaze collies are a doggie SAS, stormtroopers whose ambushes and skirmishes are the means to an end which is the total domination of everything that intrudes or encroaches on their territory. And that, unfortunately, includes postbuses and everything and everyone in them. The kamikaze collies never give up and are bred totally without fear. They are also, it has to be admitted, without any road sense (or much common sense either) when out on furlough from their usual disciplined lives and working beats.

Watching them herd and regiment their flocks, bringing them down off the high hills for winter is a fine sight. As they race and circle, eyeballing any sheep which dares to stray, tongues hanging like fat red ribbons from their mouths, stomachs and tails feathering the ground, ears always at the full cock for their master's whistle, they are a rural enchantment. Watching them do likewise with a postbus, travelling lawfully down their patch, is also heart-stopping although in a rather different way. How they survive is a mystery. There should, by rights, be at least as many squashed collies on the road as rabbits and hedgehogs. A vixen teaching them some Highway Code wouldn't come amiss at all – but then you don't find too many foxes chasing after postbuses. Foxes know you can't eat postbuses.

Stuart Mcleod-Slater

However kamikaze collies refuse to believe this, as any postbus repair shop will testify. Bumpers, tyres and bodywork all carry the teeth marks of their perverse obsession and Bob Shaw, in Forres, would particularly like it mentioned that he isn't personally given to munching petrol caps, but one of the collies up the forest road is hell-bent on nothing else for a snack.

Further south in Royal Deeside, at Ballater, Stuart McLeod-Slater's morning would not be complete

61

without his joust with the four-legged (although God knows how he's managed to keep the full quartet) rural guerrilla who lives at the golf course and whose personal Holy Grail is Stuart's bus. He stalks it. He chases it. He flings himself in front of it. It is only on account of Stuart's driving that he has not been removed long since to that great kennel in the sky. Stuart blames it on the fact that dogs are allegedly colour blind.

'He can't see its red, can he?' said Stuart in his own mongrel tones which meld Guildford to Deeside. 'So he thinks it's just a great big sheep which needs to be kept in order.'

Although the collies usually work alone, sometimes they team up, form battalions and work pincer movements. One on each side, crouched low ready to pounce at the first and frequently every chance. Perhaps they could show it on television: 'One Postbus and Its Dogs'?

Not that they are the only suicidal animals on the postbus beat. There are always the collies' charges, the sheep themselves who, according to Liz Stewart, spend their whole day on Islay waiting patiently by the side of the unfenced machair for her bus coming down the road to the miniature airport, so that they can fling themselves underneath her wheels. She swears that for the rest of the time they keep themselves to themselves, well out of harm's way, chomping the coarse grass and ignoring all other traffic until they sight her bus, when they immediately queue up in orderly lines to throw themselves, one by one, in front of Minnie Bus.

As we shared a companionable moan, I told her there were worse things than sheep determined on suicide out there. Some were bent on murder ,or so John Doolan confided to me the day he and I drove in the Peugeot Estate on a perfect afternoon between Biggar and Scotland's highest village, Leadhills. John was still recovering from being ambushed by a ram which had chased him almost over the English border as he attempted to deliver a farmer's letter.

'It was probably his subsidy cheque too,' he said with feeling.

John's regulars, who live hard on their unproductive acres, can be as thrawn as their blackfaced flocks. There was the time he tried to deliver a recorded delivery letter, which has to be signed for. For days John traipsed back and forwards, down the long, rutted farm road until finally, after a weary wait he at last found his man.

'I sign nothing,' said the farmer and slammed the door in John's face. After many more days of negotiation, he finally agreed and wrote, with a flourish, 'X'.

Meanwhile, hanging in the canteen in the Post Office at Forres, there is the Director's framed citation awarded to postman Jake Wright in October 1992 for, it says, 'Saving a member of the public from being attacked by a mad animal (a ram) which reflects great credit on himself and the Royal Mail.'

There are also many deer – too many in rural and not-so-rural Scotland, according to those who have lost every growing thing not masticated between

There is time to appreciate the scenery from a postbus and on the Forres to Granton-on-Spey run there is much to see and wonder at, including the River Findhorn in full spate and Randolph's leap.

the rabbits' rapacious jaws. As far as sizable proportions of locals are concerned, the more deer who commit *hara kiri* in front of postbuses the better. And certainly there is increasing concern that the land cannot sustain the current numbers, together with accusations that culling is both insufficient and inefficient.

That the deer are an attraction cannot be denied. Visitors were ever anxious to see and, camcorders primed, to film them for the folks back home. And the herds make for a fine picture. Once I counted 200 hinds, quivering and panting quietly by the roadside in Glenlyon. Big bambis, huge-eyed and enchanting, waiting for the stags. Or in Ballater, waiting instead for Stuart's colleague who regularly feeds them Jaffa Cakes. Stuart isn't quite sure why it must be Jaffa Cakes and nothing else, but there it is.

Later, early in the rutting season, coming over Rannoch Moor from Pitlochry,

Bill McIntosh sat enjoying his morning break and watched as two stags fought for their droit du seigneur over the does and absolute supremacy, two fleshly, muscled juggernauts of sinew and horn, bellowing defiance at each other, antlers locked and completely oblivious to the bright red bus and its occupant.

To the sporting estates and their owners, however, the deer are simply a cash crop, another way of holding on to and paying for their acres. Down the long main street of Grantown-on-Spey, which – like so many others – is now given up to the needs of tourism (it was, I found, perfectly simple to buy luxurious hand-made chocolates but not always quite as easy to find a pound of sugar), parade the hunting and shooting corps. Tweeded, moleskinned, green-wellied and well-Barboured from end to end, these days they are as likely – probably more likely – to speak with the tongues of Italy and Germany as public school and private income. So long as they also bring in Deutschmarks and lira and can shoot in the approximate direction of the deer, no one seems particularly bothered. Just another bunch of tourists passing through with a fortnight of slaughter in mind.

Although down at the pubs, where the ghillies and gamekeepers gather for a pint and a gossip about this week's guests and temporary tenants of the lodges and big houses, they are a source of amusement and some derision as well as of income. No one is more contemptuous of the weekend or holiday sportsman than a countryman, secure in his skills, even if not entirely in his employment.

For all that, those who live off and for the huntin', shootin' and fishin' remain as class-conscious as any Victorian social climber. We may all be in the Common Market now but some of us are, at least in the eyes of the men who shepherd their charges over hill and glen, from cover to kill, who load the guns, who work the dogs, who forelock-tug (at least for a good tip), are much more common than others. And that includes all foreigners, beginning at Hadrian's Wall.

They keep a fierce defensiveness towards their beats and their vocations. It may seem at best daft and at worst downright cruel to nurture and raise with such dedication and what is a kind of love, those silly pheasant chicks whose only purpose is to fly and die for the guns.

In Islay, birds of a different feather aggravate the islanders – the ever-increasing flocks of migrant geese. In most islanders' eyes the geese are vermin. But fairly tasty vermin who should, if there was any justice at all, not be gorging themselves on the island's precious grasslands and excreting noxious droppings, but would be in their proper place – on a plate with an orange stuffed up their insides. That is undoubtedly the fate of some of them.

Even they have a better life than the two ducks I met out with Evelyn, up on the kinder parts of her run, amongst the shorn white sheep and the shorn golden fields, away from Torness, where the commuters roost in gentrified rural splendour. It was 8 a.m. and the owners had long since commuted to

their Edinburgh computers. Only the ducks, pure white waddled out to meet us, rocking their great flat feet from side to side over the green grass. Country pets left outside with only a kitchen bowl of water in which to sport and play, without even a fenced-in run or proper shelter. These were not the first brace of ducks to decorate the trim and tidy lawns. They went to the foxes as these two will also assuredly go and any that follow.

The Post Office at Achnashhen where sub postmaster, David Davenport, originally from Richmond in Surrey, watches birds, trains as well and Royal Mail.

CHAPTER SIX

COFFINS, COUCHES AND OTHER CARGO

We were driving down from Laide to Poolewe and on to Achnasheen and its station, where the trains stop on the West Highland Line and where there is a perfect, circular pond in which swim wooden ducks and a stuffed heron wades. Not that I was surprised because by then, halfway through my postbus days, I had learned not to be surprised by anything. Once I might have found abundant artificial wildfowl in the middle of some of Scotland's wilder countryside odd, but after my weeks on the road I had become used to and indeed treasured such incongruities. Not to mention being given, in my hotel, with fishing boats unloading barely a hundred yards away and in a restaurant decorated with creels and nets, a breaded, frozen, triangular fillet of something softish and white which might once have been fish, together with chips which had an even more tenuous relationship to potatoes than the orange-coated fish had to the sea.

So a pond, which would not have looked out of place in some East Anglian village, re-sited in the middle of the north-western Highlands complete with

What well dressed butchers wear over the sea in Skye.

counterfeit mallards, was no more than par for the tourist course. No more peculiar than by being introduced by Nigel Nice to a butcher who should by rights, with his immaculate striped apron and white hat, have been standing behind Harrods' meat counter rather than cutting up joints of beef and lamb in a breeze-block bunker on a mountainside close by Torrin in Skye with no visible habitation let alone customers within a cleaver's throw.

Murdo MacKenzie, who used to be a French polisher in Glasgow before he began driving the postbus down to Achnasheen asked if I had heard that the postbuses used to carry coffins up to Inversnaig, post-haste to Angus the Diver. Not, of course, as Murdo explained , and I by then expected, that Angus was a diver but the local undertaker.

Murdo said he was relieved the coffins were before his time because, in his opinion, that sort of cargo was more trouble than it was worth. First of all, what exactly *was* a coffin worth? As Murdo said, there would be terrible complications working out how much to charge.

'I mean, would it have to pay extra on the way back?' he wondered. 'When it was . . . well, occupied, like?'

Apart from which consideration you have also to think of other passengers, for Murdo's route is one of the service's most popular, used extensively by

68

both locals and tourists. Maybe the locals might be willing to bounce along the road with a coffin on board – and according to at least one former Royal Mail employee, once when coffins were a fairly regular feature of some rural routes, they were more than happy to do so, even sometimes sitting atop the coffins themselves – because they appreciate the difficulty of these things; but tourists, thought Murdo, would very likely find it a wee bit off-putting. Seeing the countryside and rural life, the slow way by postbus was one thing, but being forced to watch the scenery go by from a makeshift hearse was quite another. As Murdo said, it isn't easy – and he being a French polisher had specialised knowledge – to disguise a coffin. The shape's against the whole enterprise right from the start. Although Murdo remembered a predecessor who had done his best: 'I heard he kept a big piece of hessian and a tarpaulin under his seat. to throw over it.' As for the Postmaster (deceased) at Lochmaddy who had specifically requested in his last will and testament that the bus should be used on his final journey to meet his maker, Murdo felt he would pass on that one too.

Equally unpopular in Murdo's opinion are the ubiquitous midges. Walkers use Murdo's bus all the time, and he's more than glad to pick them up when their calves and boots give up; but the problem is that when he opens the door to let them in, the midges hitch a ride as well.

'I'm thinking,' he said, 'of applying to head office to put in a shower – or maybe a hose would do it, because the minute they get on, the midges don't stay with the hikers but make straight for fresher blood which is muggins here and I tell you, driving a bus with a cloud of midges eating you isn't a thing I'd recommend.'

No one would recommend it on Murdo's route. It is a steep run down from Laide, with and without coffins and midges, and without doubt one of the most obviously spectacular. Murdo has the lot on his route – lochs, heather and hills. There's Loch Maree and the sea and the blue mountains with their neat snow-caps, and all those perfect little tourist toy-towns which lift the heart of any traveller who comes upon them, small Highland heavens

Nature forms her own sculptures to compliment and contemplate the charms of Loch Maree.

like the twin whitewashed Gairlochs and Poolewe, where the Post Office sells glorious cakes and wonderful scones which made up, almost, for the frozen fish, while just along the road are the fabled gardens at Inverewe, with their palm trees and lush tropicana protected by the Gulf Stream and thriving nearer the North Pole than the Equator.

There have been times, though, when Murdo, or more accurately his regular passengers, wished Inverewe was less popular, especially in the summer months when they are held up by the inevitable tour buses. Or when six brawny rangers from the gardens used to take the postbus to and from work – when they climbed aboard with their equipment (and the inevitable midges) there wasn't an awful lot of room for anyone else.

'Forby,' said Jack Winship from Poolewe, who never misses his Tuesday run on Murdo's bus down to the station to catch the train which catches the bus which eventually gets him into the bookie's in Inverness just in time for the off at Kempton Park or wherever. 'They ponged something awful.' It was, he opined, something to do with the thick socks they wore, even in a steaming August, or maybe their industrial-strength wellies.

Jack, who came to the area from Glasgow twenty years ago and has never quite found the will to go home again and who works in a hotel in Poolewe, couldn't survive without his Tuesday treat on his one day off, even if it does cost him, as he hops from postbus to train and bus and back again, over £15 a trip and all before he's placed his first bet. He loves his chosen Highland home as well as the horses, regretting only the ridiculous distance between his obsessions.

'They see putting a bet on as a major sin up here,' he said, tapping the side of his nose.

Islay's postbuses don't admit to having coffins lurking under hessian tarpaulins, although they have carried some things which might, in other places, seem a mite odd but not in communities a long way from the world of shopping centres and superstores. Although, Cameron said, there is, or rather are, Roys of Bowmore. Despite the variety of choice on Islay, as well as in so many other remote places, the majority of consumers do their spending by mail order and hardly a home is without its own library of catalogues, exchanged between neighbours and as essential to country life as septic tanks and winter woollens. There is a catalogue for everything, and hardly a postbus leaves on any journey without carting something bought and sent from their

Postbus in gloaming, Barra

pages. Frocks for the masters' wives at Rannoch School. A case of something vintage and expensive down at Forres. Seedlings for a cottage and a pram for a new mother on Skye. The drivers have fetched and carried it all, although there have been times when the patience of even the most obliging of them must have been tested along with back sprain. Not to mention the matter of space, for an eleven-seat Sherpa is not a Tardis any more than postbus drivers

are necessarily Supermen. However, they do try and when one of Cameron McGhie's regulars ordered a large three-piece suite from the posh home furnishers in Glasgow, which came properly wrapped as per the regulations, there wasn't much he could do except heave it into the back as best he could and deliver it.

Carpets, he said, thinking deeply and consulting Donda MacLean, another of the drivers, were on the whole easier.

'Very true that,' agreed Donda, who was christened Donald but prefers Donda to distinguish him from too many other Donalds. 'Because, now you see, Cameron, a carpet can be rolled up but couches cannot.'

Very true, agreed Cameron. They are both, he reminded Donda, quite happy too to transport coal bunkers, although Cameron said he drew the line at the coal itself. Because, said Donda sagely, it would likely dirty the bus. I am not so sure about that other rural necessity, peat, which it was rumoured was not an entirely unknown commodity on at least some postbuses whose shape may not lend themselves happily to couches and chairs but in which a winter's supply of peat would sit snugly.

So do trees. Should anyone ever want, once more, Birnam Wood to flit to Dunsinane, I wouldn't be at all surprised to find some postbus willing to oblige. After all, on Luing, Sandy Shairp once transported the foundation of a small plantation. It was just another parcel to him, he said, and fair-dos, they were only wee trees and anyway he put paper on the seats first to keep them clean.

However dogs, the postbuses' informal, sometimes unpaid-for passengers, can cause problems for the fastidious. Jill Beamer remembers coming down from Torridon and being thumbed down by a local shepherd looking for a lift for himself and his two collies after a hard day out on the hill. Jill, herself originally from Merseyside, likes to oblige locals when she can so she took the three of them on board, not too worried because working dogs, when under the eye of their owner, are the most obedient of animals. It was just her bad luck that also on the bus that afternoon was a lady tourist carrying with her an extremely smart set of luggage. Or at least it *was* extremely smart until the sheepdogs used various pieces as scratch pads to rub off the accumulated muck of their day and growled when the tourist tried to stop them. Or possibly it was their owner, for shepherds are known to be touchy about other folk interfering with their dogs.

None the less, collies' muck is probably easier to disguise than donkey detritus which was what one of Steuart Murray's colleagues down in Kirkcudbright found himself involuntarily transporting after one of his regulars heaved a sackful of manure aboard. The driver was not at first – although that altered fairly rapidly – aware what was within the gently steaming canvas at his feet. He thought the man had murmured that it was a wee gift, something from the garden, and he fondly thought of freshly dug

73

potatoes and turnips, until he was forced to realise that he had misheard – the sack was *for* his garden, ten smelly miles further on. Old lobster creels on Skye are similarly unpopular with Nigel Nice for much the same olfactory reason, since the smell tends to linger long after the creels have departed.

Perhaps they should follow the example of the drivers in Biggar. It wasn't dogs or lobsters or even donkeys which caused their problem, but a group of people, itinerant tinkers temporarily based in the area and collectively known as the Stinkies. The drivers and the other passengers complained to head office who, it is said, after a great deal of deliberation and many meetings, decided that Stinkie or not, so long as the fare was paid they had to be carried. Regulations were more overpowering than the smell, although one small concession was granted: all affected drivers were allowed a special payment for air fresheners. Something, I did ever so occasionally feel, as I caught yet another whiff of armpit, which might usefully be made standard postbus equipment. It's all those layers of clothing worn against the country chills, for people tend to wear more than in towns and thicker, woollier things which, when wet, dry off noisomely in the buses' often-cramped, fetid air.

Most of the cargo carried is more conventional, possibly more acceptable, and much less exotic than trees and coffins and three-piece suites. It consists of everyday items like morning rolls and general groceries, an old lady's messages, another's designer tracksuit from a Sunday supplement. Sometimes it is a contracted service paid for by shops and their remoter customers, and other times it is something rather less formal, a favour: so if the girl from the garage in Lochearnhead asks Robert Ferguson coming down from Killin to take her film to be developed at the end of his run in Callander, he is only too happy to oblige, just as Allan Gallacher will carry prescriptions up to Tighnabruaich for housebound OAPs who can't make it down to the dispensary. All of it done in a without matter-of-fact way, with an absence of fuss or bother, because the postbus and its drivers are seen as part and parcel of these communities where neighbour still looks out for neighbour.

This applies to their foibles as well as their frailties. The desperate gentleman in Skye, a dead ringer for Hemingway, an oldish man of the sea in his khaki shorts, beard, paunch and sandals, who had planned a small celebration with a congenial chum while his wife was temporarily otherwise engaged would have had to make other, more abstemious plans for his evening if Nigel Nice hadn't done the necessary down at the off-licence in *Greigsland* Broadford. Oh the agony when he thought Nigel had forgotten and the *farm on the* ecstasy when Nigel at last, ritual teasing done, found the discreetly packaged *Lockerbie run*

supplies.

It all takes time, but time is usually found and regained somewhere. People know that it's how they run things in the country. It makes the job more interesting, the drivers said, even if Tommy Devlin in Aberfeldy, rushing cheese up to a hotel for its bar lunch and Welsh Rarebit, wasn't entirely joking when he said that there are days when he thinks that he and his fellow drivers are just glorified message boys with buses.

They are also often the newspaper boy or girl as well, dropping off the papers. Like Robin Laing in Linlithgow dropping off the broadsheets at the smart houses, and Tommy with his tabloids in Aberfeldy, although Tommy says that it's usually only in the estates that people expect to get their papers delivered. Country life is expensive. Sometimes I would get off the bus to stretch my legs and my knowledge and amble through the local shops and price the more common groceries – cereal, soap powder, baked beans and toothpaste – and invariably they cost a penny or two more per tin and box than at home. At least the papers, even when flown in by the Paraffin Budgie always cost the same.

Papers are a necessity of life in the country, and at every stop where they were dropped off people waited impatiently, scanning the roads for their daily fix of print. Bill McIntosh recognised their importance when he surrendered his own *Courier* to Mrs Mary Wilson, off on the postbus in her neat green tweeds to visit the daughter who lives up in the farm on the edge of the pipeline at Rannoch Power Station and who, Mrs Wilson says, will kill her for sure if she forgets to bring a paper with her. It seems most people might possibly make do without milk for a day but not their papers, for tea and coffee can come black at a pinch but a newspaper cannot be missed. Even the post itself – especially if it's nothing but bills – is sometimes less welcome in the morning than newspapers. But not, however, on account of their news. Those well-honed leaders and carefully composed columns, the readers can do without; it's the times of the TV programmes and the numbers which will automatically set their videos which are so eagerly awaited.

One delivery that Stuart MacLeod-Slater and I made deep into the bowels of Glenshee struck me as particularly odd. We drove down a long track, far too rough and unready ever to be called anything like a road. They had told me back at the Post Office in Ballater that Stuart's run was likely to be both one of the most beautiful and the least comfortable of my journeys. They were not wrong, as Annette can confirm.

Annette was a South African, an Africaaner on holiday from Pretoria, and all day she travelled in the back, crouched down with the mail bags, clinging to her camcorder, shooting off miles of film out the back window while Stuart and I rode in cushioned comfort in front. Annette, Stuart and I rattled and bumped down this endless rut-ridden path and at its eventual conclusion came to a house whose kennels, although falling down, were in somewhat better repair than the house itself. The owner was waiting, watching out for us, impatient at his peeling door, desperate for his specially ordered literature. It was not a newspaper nor even a DIY manual but a hot-off-the-press copy of a glossy magazine: not just any old magazine either, but that apologia, bible and directory of the well-heeled and vacuous – *Hello!*

As I said, wooden ducks on the pond at Achnasheen are not really that odd at all.

There may no longer be telegrams and telegram boys with leather pouches slung over their shoulders but at least there are still paper boys like 11 year old Michael Thorpe at Hightae getting on their bikes.

Scott's View

CHAPTER SEVEN

TOURISTS AND OTHER HAZARDS

The more I saw of it, the more I appreciated that it was altogether a most peculiar job, this being a postbus driver – possibly only split personalities need apply. Those who can spend long tracts of time completely on their own with nothing but the passing scenery and a radio for company but who can, in an instant, at the wave of a passenger's whim, switch into the tourists' informative guide as well as the regulars' friend and familiar.

At least the locals don't expect a running commentary and history lesson, although they would be disappointed if there wasn't constant hot and cold running gossip. Tourists are different because tourists are on holiday and want to be entertained and educated. Some drivers manage it better than others but then, as they kept telling me, some of them have to.

I was up beside the driver and it was raining hard, the sort of weather they euphemistically call 'soft' in these parts. On the radio Gene Pitney was 'Twenty-Four Hours from Tulsa' and we were thirty minutes from a cup of something hot. We glimpsed the man at the same time although he was half

The postbuses have their official fan club and many more unofficial fans including postie Andrew Foulcher from Wellingborough on a postman's holiday spotting the wee red buses.

hidden, standing at the side of the road in the dirt beside the sheep, with the rain drizzling down his all-weather army surplus anorak, a small waterfall creeping through his beard, dripping relentlessly into his vest, high-velocity binoculars in hand and wearing an expression of pure bliss. He was oblivious to life's discomforts because he was near journey's end and close to a personal nirvana, as he completed his quest and bagged his prey. I recognised the breed instantly, just another kind of twitcher.

And so it was that I met a birdwatcher of an entirely different genus, my very first member of the Ride the Royal Mail Postbus Club, who spot with passion not the corncrake or the lesser grebe but the scarlet-plumaged Sherpa and brighter red Land Rover. But why, I asked, when the driver relented, stopped and allowed him on board, why the fascination with vans, which is, after all, what postbuses are? He told me his story. Once upon another hobby he had been a train-spotter who one summer holiday came north to see the engines chugging up and down the West Highland Line. He was on his bike and toiling perpendicularly up beyond Callander on his way to Ardrishaig, when, there in front of him, was his first postbus.

'I stuck out my hand,' he said, his eyes misty with the memory of that day, 'just to wave, you know, like you do – and it *stopped*. Well, that was it really. I mean, I ask you, you can't stick out your hand at a train and it pulls up, any old where, just for you, does it?'

So in an instant he took up with his new loves, the postbuses. Not that the man is anything like alone with his obsession. Ben Jenkins, treasurer, chairman and onlie begetter of the entire enterprise, runs the club from deepest Devon where members are restricted to a hundred.

There is certainly one native admirer: Jack Wahlberg, late of Aberdeen though he now works for the Royal Mail in south-east England, is a long-time fan, if not fanatic. Along with David Cott, Jack is presently engaged on an odyssey which made mine seem very insignificant indeed, to travel, over three years, on every single postbus route. For love, certainly, but for money too, raising impressive amounts of cash for the Cancer Research Fund along their way. Jack and David are also the proud owners of the only pair of privately owned postbuses, pensioned off now from active service but lovingly maintained and restored, two of those old, original, much photographed and admired Commers with their white roofs and bone-rattling suspension.

Neither is above admiring the newer models, or driving them, which was how Stuart MacLeod-Slater came to find himself in the back of his Land Rover between Braemar and Ballater when Jack came calling. Wasn't it odd for a driver to become, however briefly, a passenger? I enquired. Stuart hesitated and confessed that he couldn't say, really, because he had fallen fast asleep somewhere beyond Glenshee.

The National Trust's Catherine Ross picks flowers in the Prior's garden at Melrose Abbey.

I suspect Jack and David have yet to visit Neil Hall down in Melrose, since he has carried no new passengers for eighteen months. Tourists tend to miss his run, which is strange because it travels slowly by and journeys through some extremely touristy places: Sir Walter Scott as well as Mary, Queen of Scots both definitely stepped and slept here. Although the tourists photograph the bus and pose beside it in Melrose, they seldom take the trip to those other, more secret gardens of Lilliesleaf and soporific Bowden Cross, through the high-hedged country roads and past obese sheep gorging themselves on lush pastureland. Which is a pity because there can be few better ways of appreciating some of Scotland's gentler countryside than from the high seat of a postbus.

Hamish McDonald, on the run to Cove only has to find room for one traveller in his estate car and not 15 German rucksack laden tourists.

There are, of course, others routes which are more popular and which are seldom without their tourist quota. Nigel Nice on Skye and Robert Ferguson, who drives between Killin and Callander, seldom have much time for solitary contemplation, at least in summer when the visitors crowd their buses.

Although most of the drivers would like the service to be better advertised, there have been times when this is not entirely true. Like the occasion when Murdo MacKenzie's colleague Jamie Johnston, driving between Redpoint and Gairloch found seventeen German tourists (and their rucksacks) waiting expectantly for him to take them back to Kinlochewe. They had been told about the postbuses, they said, by their own Tourist Office, and advised not to miss this quaint transport. What seemed to have been omitted in Munich was the information that Jamie's postbus is more accurately a postcar, in reality a Peugeot Estate, maximum number of passengers four thin or three fat, and absolutely no room at all for tourist impedimenta. Jamie eased in five of the slimmer Fräuleins. When, the others enquired politely, would he be back for them? 'Tomorrow,' he replied, equally politely.

Bob Shaw was polite, too, to three Germans who drove with him one particularly hot summer's day. He remembers it well, not only because a hot day in Forres is not something easily forgotten but this one was made even more memorable when the two girls stripped down to their bras on the road to Braemoray. As Bob says, it was fine by him and anyway they were foreign and foreigners do things which the respectable burghers and natives of Forres might not. Besides, their English was as good as his German and sign language, I agreed – once I thought about it and indeed tried it myself – is not perhaps quite the best way in which to encourage people to put their blouses on. Getting the wrong idea would be only too easy and so Bob just kept his eyes on the road and got on with his own and the Royal Mail's business. The only problem, he said, came when he stopped for a delivery and the ladies decided to get out and indulge in a spot of topless sunbathing in one of the forest's sun-warmed glades. They didn't seem to understand that he couldn't wait indefinitely until those parts he was heroically ignoring were uniformly tanned and that unless they climbed back on the bus immediately they would be returning, bra-less, to Forres on foot. Which might have been fine in their part of Germany but wasn't really something they were ready for in Bob's part of Scotland.

In Dunoon, down by the pier where the fairy lights shine bravely on, even at 6.50 a.m. in a Force Ten gale, Allan Gallacher meets the first ferry coming across the slapping waves from Gourock. Once it would have disgorged the Americans sailors who manned the Polaris submarines, and who for twenty-odd years fired the local economy and supported fleets of taxis and DIY mini-cabs. All departed now. Not that it affects Allan particularly, for the sailors never used his bus and although he knows that there are those who miss their money – and the jobs they created – he for one does not regret their going. He is happy that more conventional tourists are slowly returning to the Cowal Peninsula and that those black lozenges of the Cold War, with their secret sub-maritime entrances and exits, no longer creep up and down the Holy Loch.

Allan prefers the peace in every sense. His route up to Tighnabruaich is

considered by many, in and out of the Royal Mail, to be the one of the most beautiful. As far as Allan's concerned, his run is quite definitely *the* most beautiful with no rivals nor dissent allowed, even from the islands and Braemar. He stopped his bus on the road high above the Kyles of Bute and Loch Striven where the buzzards fly proud and where the scarlet and purple fuchsia promiscuously tumbles and blooms, above a perfect pattern of islets and sea and coast. 'There,' he ordered me. 'Look at all that.' Ozymandias in a postbus.

In Barra Niall MacPherson has the whole business of informative tourist-guiding down to the finest of arts – the perfumery here, the Viking settlements over there and the new community school outside Castlebay are all meticulously itemised, ticked off his internal list as efficiently as he delivers the mail. Each is given its history and a comment or two, not always complimentary. Excuses for the island, if something fails to charm or live up to his advance billing, are effortlessly manufactured out of the ether. Two visitors dropped off at Seal Island around noon complain that, contrary to their expectations, they hadn't seen so much as a single flipper,

Polaris may have left Dunoon but the postbus still remains to meet the ferry from Gourock.

'Ah well,' Niall ruminated thoughtfully. 'They'll have gone off for their lunch at this time of day now, won't they?'

And they too went off docilely, satisfied, for theirs.

Although once, as we discussed that year's earlier disaster in Shetland, when the oil tanker *Braer* had gone aground, there was a rare flash, an explosion of anger. We were looking out at the Minch which was rolling and prettily foaming in front of us and where, despite the known and documented dangers, the giant supertankers continually sail its narrow, treacherous channels. I asked Niall the knowledgeable seaman, rather than Niall the relaxed postbus driver, if he thought a *Braer* could happen off Barra.

'Of course it could . . . indeed it will, if they don't keep the tankers out of here. We've been telling them that for years.'

Then he put the mask back and we returned to the banalities once more, to safe, innocuous, tourist talk again.

Stopping for his tea at Gaur, overlooking Loch Rannoch, Bill McIntosh philosophised on the more general problem of foreigners.

'Ah well,' he said, 'sometimes, you see, they can't make me out and sometimes I can't make them out – and now sometimes that's an advantage.'

Something which some foreigners found very difficult to make out on the day I drove with Bill was Rannoch School, the establishment founded by two former Gordonstoun masters and run on a similar hearty, healthy and unhedonistic basis. The foreigners in question were from East Germany and their command of English was a tribute to that country's own educational standards but was not quite able to cope with the concept of public meaning very private indeed when prefixed to the word 'school'. And then Rannoch does not look anything like a school. To begin with, it has bred its very own suburbia, its little satellite city of bijou bungalows in which the staff live with their flower gardens, children's toys and pedigree dogs all gated behind their fences.

Beyond them and the private fire station and tender lies the main school building, which is a clotted cream confection of a castle, looking the way most of us expect a castle should look, down to its last arrow slit and crenellate, indeed so perfect that one fears it must be MacDisney. There is also, unfortunately, the square, brutal new building for the girls more recently admitted as pupils to this arcadian academe, which no doubt goes well enough with the bungalows. From one of its square windows a bra dangled and danced incongruously in the bracing air.

In front and all around are the vacuumed rugby pitches and tennis courts, all created in the middle of some of the last few remaining acres of the Caledonian Forest. The end of Bill's run and miles from anywhere, its own little kingdom, ordered, lovely and remote, with birdsong and red squirrels in the trees, a tuck shop in an outhouse and Latin declension chorusing from a classroom.

We had picked the Germans up at Rannoch Station, which in the way of these things is on the moor and some way from Rannoch village itself, but it is also a station out of *The Railway Children*, old-fashioned and comforting, reaching across the years, reminding those who visit how railways used to be. It is a tourist trap of the nicest sort, where people come to tramp the moor or catch the train on its single spectacular track north, or simply to stand and stare and take a picture or two before climbing back into their cars and driving home again.

If they do cross over the high, iron-trellised bridge, they will find some of the best baking for miles around. Hiding in Mrs Eunice McLelland's modest little tearoom on the platform, with the hygiene certificate on the wall and the visitors' book by the door, underneath their glass cloches, are the most luscious cakes after which my taste-buds have ever over-salivated.

Calorie and cholesterol cocktails which alone are worth a stroll to Rannoch Station. Not to mention the breakfasts on which walkers and hikers

Mrs Eunice McLelland displays her home made bounty and possibly the best cakes in the little tea room on the platform at Rannoch Station.

and those who are neither fall with glad and hungry cries: fried eggs, fried ham, fried bread, fried everything but fresh and tasty and all cooked in a tiny kitchen in which it would be hard to swing a mouse. Not of course that there are any. Mrs McLelland caters daily for Bill's elevenses and upwards of sixty other people in between advising train travellers on the cheapest way to Mallaig and beyond.

'Buy a day return there and a single back,' I think she said and it made sense at the time.

Mrs McLelland also manages to ignore completely the low-flying jets screaming out of the horizon and down through the scudding clouds to within feet of her and her feasts.

'Has war broken out?' asked an American, not altogether jokingly, cowering into his new Burberry with the price tag still on the sleeve and nervously ducking as they dived in mock combat above us. The station apparently makes a useful target for them and so does a red postbus. If they don't stop buzzing him soon, I suggested to Bill that he indents the Royal Mail for a tin or two of camouflage paint. In the meantime, there are far worse and few better air-raid shelters in which to await the cessation of hostilities than Mrs McLelland's teashop.

Bill is also thinking of applying for an Equity card because, he explained, brushing the crumbs from his uniform, I was his third journalist this month. Not that he minded and was becoming very adept at posing with his bus, looking pensive or purposeful or whatever the photographer wanted, to order. Television crews, too, came from abroad as well as from home. The school children on Skye who travel down to Broadford with Nigel Nice were becoming rather blasé about their performances, including one for a TV station in Germany. And in Dunbar, possibly the most photographed and filmed, if only because of its fame as the first Scottish route, Molly Lafferty, that first passenger, has almost as many cuttings as a minor soap star and her script and lines as pat and as perfect too.

Much later, to recuperate from too many weeks spent sitting in postbuses, I flew on holiday to Dublin by Aer Lingus, for something entirely different. Somewhere over the Irish Sea I flicked through the in-flight magazine, *Cara*, and there, suddenly, was Bill McIntosh again and Mrs McLelland too, in full colour, cakes and all – one of those other journalist's work and the magazine's main feature. I reached for a very stiff gin. I needed it. And another. After all, it is one thing you cannot get on a postbus. Yet.

En route, Kirkubright to Borgue.

CHAPTER EIGHT

REGULARS AND THE DEMON GOSSIP

If there is a hidden subtitle and subtext to this book, it is that phrase heard at every stop from the eager lips of every regular: 'I don't know what we'd do without it.' They said it over and over again until it became, in my head, the postbus mantra. When locals saw me on their particular route, my notebook and pen to hand, asking questions, there was always the worry expressed openly or covertly that I might be some official, threatening the service, taking it away from them.

For many of the regulars had already seen an awful lot go: their youth – because the majority were not young; their small communities – which had shrunk and shrivelled around them, even as their own flesh had shrivelled and their very bones had shrunk; their children – for they had grown up and gone away as the industries which might once have employed them disappeared; their transport – many were too old or too poor to drive cars, while trains and buses were either gone or came infrequently. Even the landscapes and the little townscapes within which they lived were changing and evolving and nothing was what it seemed any more. They were passing their days and the end of their lives in places where almost every building, from church to library to school to shop and station, had been transformed into something else, and seldom something beneficial to them – a hotel, a holiday home, a new business, a restaurant, a ruin. All the former certainties had largely dissolved around them, which was why they cherished anything which remained. Like their particular postbus, about which many felt proprietorial, as if it was their very own.

Unwillingly to school by postbus

Not that all the regulars are old. The postbus can be the schoolbus too. On Luing and Skye, at least, Sandy Shairp and Nigel Nice now drive the children of the first children they took backwards and forwards, willingly or otherwise, to school. But for the most part, those who use the service are towards the end rather than the beginning of their lives, lives which are made a little better by the postbus, whose regular comings and goings keep them in touch and give them a means to shop, to have their hair done, to visit friends, to place a bet or go to the pub. The regulations do not allow alcohol to be consumed, carried or catered for in any way. Like cigarette smoking, it is something strictly forbidden. It made its pernicious way on board none the less, although usually internally after a convivial session with cronies in the local hostelries. I became quite adept, on the afternoon runs, at heaving those who had indulged unwisely and too well up the high step and on to their seats. On the whole they were absolutely no trouble at all, although seat belts would perhaps have been useful on the rougher patches. I was told loudly, if very soberly, by one Angus, that he wished he could be, but that getting drunk and obstreperous on the old age pension was near impossible: 'It's a damned disgrace, so it is.'

In Lockerbie Mrs Buckley uses the bus three times every week. 'I couldn't do without it. I come in from St Ann's for shopping and to enjoy a drink.' There was something brave and charming and indomitable about people like her, with her bad legs and her meagre shopping, still making the best of things and too old to bother much about what other people thought of her but still young enough to enjoy herself.

Some passengers don't have much time for sitting and staring. Mrs Sarah Gillespie climbed on at Gairloch, hitching a hurl, she explained in an accent fashioned in far-away Glasgow, to the doctor's down the road. She was in a hurry because she runs a B & B and hadn't, she told me, with some

Mrs Sara Gillespie who has retired to Gairloch from Glasgow an found a who new career a a B and landlady. O course he visitors com by postbu

90

The Isle of Luing and its inhabitants, including the Crackin, otherwise known Hugh MacLean have a style which is definitely all their own.

satisfaction, had a free day since June. Although technically retired since she moved up here five years ago, her wee business is doing just fine, thank you very much. And, of course, she had to say she couldn't do without the bus at all. Not only for hurling to the doctor's but because it also brings up her family from the station at Achnasheen and a fair number of customers as well, mostly climbers and walkers. Foreigners, she said, mostly from England but from further away too. 'All nice folk,' she assured me.

On the bus they also remembered the old days which were not necessarily good, but of course they regretted the passing of some of it. Most of all the sense of safety and security, and being able to leave doors unlocked. Now there are the Neighbourhood Watch signs and burglar alarm boxes everywhere, even in the remotest corners where burglars would surely have to wear climbing boots. And they sighed over the passing of the time when they knew the name and history and family of everyone within their area. Although it seemed to me that they still did.

But they did not sentimentalise or romanticise any privations of their younger lives. Just before we reached her daughter at the farm by the power station at Rannoch, Mrs Wilson pointed up the hill to the ruins of the house in which she had been born, now replaced by one of the ubiquitous kit bungalows. Mrs Wilson has no doubt about which is preferable because she also knows what it is like to live in a house where the only running water ran in the nearby burn. Which may, on that pleasant September morning, have sparkled and tumbled past in the sun but which, when it was her bath and bathroom, froze the soap and chilled every bone. There is nothing very appealing either about making the choice at night between an en suite chamber pot or an outside dry privy. Mrs Wilson's family didn't have what she called the amenities until the family moved down to the village, by which time Mrs Wilson was well into her teens. She remembers her mother when they moved into the new house: She was aye at the sink, up to her elbows in it. Oh, we used to laugh that we couldn't get her out of it, she was that thrilled at having it all on tap.'

Among the acknowledged comforts and joys of the postbus was the chance to gossip. There is an open slot which is let into the wired metal grille that separates driver from passengers. On Luing, Sandy Shairp says it's very useful for feeding bananas to his regulars, his human zoo. I think he was joking but then with Sandy one can never be entirely sure about such things. However, technically, and more usually, the slot is for the collection of fares and the distribution of tickets. It is also through this space that the day's gossip is batted backwards and forwards in the never- ending game.

Postbuses are fuelled at least as much by rumour and hearsay as by diesel and engines and at every stop they are tanked up with yet more tales, true and very possibly untrue but whoever lets anything as irrelevant as the truth get in the way of a good story? Not I. I want to believe, like the locals, that the man in Forres who declared to the authorities that he'd a ghost in his bedroom, which was terrifying the life out of him, only decided he was haunted when he found out they were building new council houses.

'He said it was in the wardrobe at first until he remembered it was a good wardrobe – it was left him by his wife's auntie – then the ghost moved to the bathroom.'

I wanted to know all about the new laird's lady.

'She worked in a shop. In the *underwear* department, I hear, but he sent her to elocution lessons in Glasgow. She wears black nighties.'

Gossip and local scandal have always been the stuff of small communities, and those are the ones largely served by the postbuses. Besides, for a mile or so, up a glen and down a rural road, do not the buses themselves become small, mobile communities in which the town crier is, more often than not, the driver? But a town crier with infinite tact who knows when to stay mute. They wouldn't last long in the job if they didn't because they are trusted. They have to be. There is nothing about their passengers they do not know. Small things like holidays and birthdays and larger ones of death and disaster. Just as the drivers, like every postman, know a great deal too about those who may not use the bus itself but whose post is delivered by it.

Postmen know everything.

It isn't the local bank manager who is aware first of someone's money troubles but the posties, dropping off final demands, those buff envelopes with the menacing windows and the threatening summonses. Every problem and most pleasures, too, are apparent. So they know who's been caught speeding, picked up a traffic ticket in a town or failed to pay their TV licence. They know who gets the wedding invitation and who does not, with a consolation prize of the crumbly cake in its frilled white box to come when the festivities and honeymoon are over. Feuds, vendettas and undying enmities, I learned, have been built on smaller slights.

Those who deliver the post know them all. They are first to know when a son or daughter or husband stops writing or when a love affair sours, when there are no more letters signed with a loving kiss to be delivered and impatiently ripped from the postman's hand before there is time for it to rattle through the letterbox. They know when someone is seen scurrying early out of an address to which their mail does not go, and can with confidence predict that a marriage is finished and divorce proceeding about to begin. Those men and women, sitting up with the post beside them and the passengers behind, in the end find out everything that is worth finding out and an awful lot that is not.

By the end of my journeyings, a co-opted irregular regular, I began to know a great deal too as they tossed the chat back and forward between themselves and the drivers. I heard about the second wife who made a bonfire of her predecessor's clothes. A good cashmere jumper was rescued from the flames and is even now keeping someone else's lawful wedded wife warm on colder mornings on the bus.

I saw what happened when the farmer sent his wife to her sister's while he spent a quiet, congenial evening with the girlfriend young enough to be his granddaughter, and they slept in and the wife returned early. We gave her a lift back in the bus together with a clean hankie to wipe her tears. Men, we agreed, weren't worth it – dogs were better and more faithful companions.

Nor were the incomers spared; indeed it was obligatory to find out all about every new resident.

'Your dad looks very nice,' said one of the school children brightly to a small bouncy girl with the city's pallor, an English accent and a too-new school sweatshirt.

'Oh, no,' she said, eager to explain. 'He's not my dad. My dad says he's my mum's fancy man. My dad, he lives with my auntie now.'

Oh yes indeed, sex and lies and videotapes too. Although the latter at least are more likely to be Disney than dirty; what with television reception unreliable where mountains are high and weather unpredictable, videos are popular and handed on, like gossip itself, from person to person or via the bus. They were particularly annoyed about not being able to watch TV properly in Kinloch Rannoch. It was around the nearby Perthshire town of Blair Atholl that *Strathblair* – the BBC series of 1940s rural life and hard times – was set, and sizable numbers of locals had been recruited as extras. Like any eager thespian they were more than anxious to know if their scenes had been left in or dumped on the cutting room floor. Deciphering this through the electronic white snow and multicoloured dots which was what most of their sets received was not easy. So, after the general iniquities of being required to pay the full licence fee for an imperfect service had been kicked around, they moved on to particularities.

Mrs Holly, mainstay of the village, she told me, and of the postbus, was very irritated because until her daughter sent up the video she couldn't be sure who had or had not been chosen to play a bride's upper-class father in a significant *Strathblair* episode. She was almost certain it was one of the white settlers.

'And if it was him, he was only chosen,' she confided to Janet McGregor on our way down to Pitlochry, 'because of that Cambridge accent of his. Even though he only had the one word.'

Strathblair, I thought, might have been more of a success if they'd based it in a 1990s postbus, its lives and deaths. Coffins may no longer travel by bus, but that old grim reaper was a fairly regular passenger. No one – as far as I know – actually died en route but news of others who had met their maker was ever present and frequently discussed. In an elderly age group that was not entirely surprising and, as one of them said, a good funeral was really about all he had to look forward to these days. I don't think he was talking about his own, but one doesn't like to ask these things.

Not that death was particularly feared. What was dreaded was the halfway house, the Home with the capital H. That was the real terror, the fate worse than death that stalked them. They wanted to live and to die in their own homes before being carried in their coffins to their own churchyards where their relatives lay and where there would be the familiar names of friends and neighbours all around. It was not hard to understand why. For

Mary Hogg and her shopping trolley not doing without the postbus on her way home to Borland after a morning's shop in Lockerbie.

there was something unworldly and beautiful in these final resting places, with their grassed-over graves and old, sunken, mossy headstones, frequently indecipherable, walled in beside parish churches. Usually the kirkyards, in the custom of these places, were set outwith the villages and townships, a part of but also apart from them, generally overlooking the sea or the fields, the places where the majority who lay down in its earth would have earned their daily bread, fishing on the boats and working on the farms.

There was also much that was melancholy and forlorn. I wandered one afternoon through MacPherson's kirkyard between Kelso and Nenthorn. A quiet, lovely place but sadness percolated its soul. Under those strong old trees were buried too many young lives, lost too early – the children, the babes and their mothers who died at their birth before knowing each other – all dead before their time.

Many of the graveyards have become surplus to requirements because there is no one left living who will die and leave their bones there. They have become rural mausoleums commemorating these cleared communities and deserted places.

Sandy Paterson's route passes through Lockerbie. I didn't, at first, realise the significance. It had been a pleasant ride, no more, no less much like many others I had taken. The usual regulars, the amiable, aimless gossip about grandchildren and chiropody and other matters medical. Operations, past and present, were always discussed with relish and with an intimate detail which quite often left me feeling that there were times when I had gone a postbus too far. Varicose veins were the speciality in Dunoon and piles a problem in Laide, and kidney stones, hysterectomies and prostates accompanied me through all the ferns and forests of Tayside, while constipation was everywhere. It was largely bunions and falling arches in Lockerbie, with elastic bandages versus support stockings until we had left Mrs Davidson with her daughter and Sandy had carted Mary's buggy up the postal path.

Then, for the run back down to Lockerbie, it was just Sandy and me. We crossed back towards the A74, with its roadworks without end and its constant noise, but away from the machines with their eternal digging and the vehicles moving at high speed, it was almost abnormally still. I asked Sandy if anything much ever happened on this route, in this halfway land caught between England and Scotland, in the borderlands but not really of the Borders. Sandy thought a while and then, obliging, stopped to show me the Wynholm Bridge where another driver had bent over to look at the trout below and had lost all his keys.

'That's all the excitement I can remember,' he said, 'but that's the way I like it.'

I wrote the story down dutifully and we climbed back on the bus. Sandy turned on the radio as we climbed up to Bankshill School to lift any children in need of a ride home. We were all talked out and were both half listening to the news when the voice said, 'Scottish lawyers were in Libya today, interviewing the men accused of the Lockerbie bombing.' Then I remembered that dreadful things had happened here, something beyond excitement.

'Over there,' Sandy said conversationally, without explaining more and pointing up to our left, 'over there is the field where the nose landed.' That picture seen in every paper and sent around the world to every country and into every consciousness. He stopped the postbus outside the memorial, at the kirkyard, in whose old gravedigger's hut they have made a shrine. Sandy has stopped here often before, alone, and many times more when he has brought the relatives of those who perished so violently near this peaceful place. It is a plain, small building, rough stone and smooth wood and artificial flowers. I went in and looked at the leather-bound books which, in penned, careful copperplate are recorded the names and small biographies of all the dead.

The Lockerbie Memorial Gardens commemorating the tragic crash of Flight 101 in December 1988.

Country roads crossing and meeting the postbus to Lockerbie.

Beside it is another book in which visitors had inscribed their own names. There were those like me, the curious, the passing who came and signed the book, in respect and temporary remembrance and sorrow, but detached, impersonal. And there were those others who had lost their sons and daughters, husbands and wives, fathers, mothers and friends. A company of strangers who had died together and whose relatives came together and mourned them in that little plain hut and who were perhaps comforted. They left messages: 'Hi – well, here I am again, son', which were neither detached nor impersonal and would prick tears out of stone.

Sandy and I climbed back on the bus and Sandy said that people didn't like to talk about it much. If it hadn't been for that news, he said, he would never have shown me the memorial and in truth he was glad when people like me didn't bring it up. He didn't like to speak of it himself much, not least because the plane had come down only feet away from his sister's farm. We went silently on down the hill to Lockerbie where I forbore to ask him to show me the Gardens of Remembrance and the houses which have now replaced those which disappeared into earth and flame that December night in 1988. But I do not think I shall not forget Flight 103 so easily and so blithely again.

Lockerbie delivery office.

CHAPTER NINE

POST OFFICES AND POSTBOXES

In Biggar I found myself suddenly returned to the dear, half-forgotten days of my childhood. It was the ticket machines that did it. One glance at those magnificent leather and metal contraptions with their clips and punches and the big shiny handle and I was back in Glasgow, on the trams in which I used to rattle back and forwards to school. For here, in this pleasant little country town, in its Post Office, in these high-tech days of the 1990s, there they were – time machines, tumbling me down into the low-tech 1950s again.

But sadly, without their conductresses attached (I suppose there must have been conductors too on the trams but they have escaped my memories), those big sonsy women who wore them, double-belted across chests, chests which were themselves as robust as their magical machines and which looked as if they had been permanently riveted into WXX iron brassieres down in some Clyde yard – for ships were still built on the river in my green Glasgow days.

Here, the machines were altogether more mundane, less impressive, as are nearly all recollections from childhood, just another part of the postbus driver's kit, not even worn but dumped wherever there was room, more usually the floor. But far better, I thought, to end their days here, in use, rather than melted down for scrap.

My heart lifted at that first sighting. I was to see more, in fact on every route where Strathclyde's massive writ runs. As with that Region's obsession with public lavatories in the most obscure places, it was not entirely apparent why Strathclyde alone clung to its ticket machines. Although there were times, aesthetics and memories aside, when I was grateful for both.

I saw the inside of an awful lot of Post Offices on my journey too, in all shapes and sizes and in all disguises. I had not realised their diversity before. There was the one in Eccles which looked like a shed, possibly because it was indeed a shed, through Mrs McDougall's garden gate and up her path, past the flowers to stamps, pensions paid out and a few bars of chocolate for sale. In the porch of the old lodge house at Stichill the PO scales sat on the windowsill beside a vase of fresh-cut blooms from the herbaceous border outside, with forms and leaflets tucked into the corner where umbrellas and macintoshes might have been more expected. Some were little more than a counter at the back of a shop. Giros, family allowance and post dealt with along with the half-pounds of caramels, a packet of crisps and a birthday card for Auntie Jean. Or village shops like the one in Dalton where big glass jars of boilings, humbugs and treacle toffees marched in rows in the window, old-fashioned sweets displayed in the old fashioned way.

Meanwhile, in Ceres in Fife the Post Office was but part of a modern supermarket, while in Kinlochewe and Skye they were very much appendages of the tourist trade – something which fitted in spare space between souvenirs, postcards, arts and crafts and the tearoom tacked on at the side. In Callander, tourified almost to termination and home to the first television *Doctor Finlay* and to woolly jumpers of very unfortunate colours, there is Hamish Menzies's private kingdom opposite the browny stone lions of the Dreadnought Hotel. It is an emporium of a Post Office, with a garden centre thrown in, stretching up one street, round the corner and into another, where passengers waiting for Robert Ferguson to take them up by Lix Toll and Killin, through the great grey rock falls at Dochart, could have whiled away the minutes restocking all their vegetable plots and flowerbeds and most of their home and wardrobes too.

They were meeting and greeting places too, small outstations, informal clubs where people gathered and chatted. In one, mothers cursed the new teacher who wanted the children to dress up, for pity's sake, as an EU country by Friday. 'But she's from Edinburgh,' one said, and of course that explained it all so they just cleared the shop out of crêpe paper and, like mothers everywhere, got on with it. In the Post Offices, in the warmth, people gossiped almost as much as they did on the bus, and when they had finished put up their hand-printed posters of forthcoming events, exchanged and marketed

The Royal Mail's official pillarboxes have their unofficial imitators dressed in scarlet. But then it is the sincerest from of flattery.

furniture and all those carefully chosen gifts now unwanted.

The buildings I liked best of all were the delivery offices, round the back, where there was one business and one business only. No sidelines, no distractions, nothing bought or sold, nothing at all beyond the matter of the safe delivery of the post, the general public kept at bay by strong locked doors and high-up bells .

I loved the smell of them – the paper, the envelopes, the string, the rubber bands and the mail bags. Even if the last are now grey and dull and made from synthetic stuff which doesn't quite carry the romance of sacking hand-sewn by guests of Her Majesty. I fantasised about what was in the parcels, lumpy, hidden surprises to be unwrapped pleasurably by other people. Most of all I enjoyed what they call in Ireland 'the crack' – the badinage, the words and insults flying back and forward, and the camaraderie of those who worked there and who knew each other well enough to tease and bait. They were always cheerful, busy places even although those within laboured while the rest of us slept.

These things were constant. No matter whether they were housed in modern, purpose-built factory-like units as in Forres and Pitlochry or in the old, stone-floored buildings of Islay and Barra, they were friendly places every one, despite some of the notices pinned up in nearly all of them. Dire warnings about the twin evils of drinking late and slacking early; workflow charts; and yet more posters about dogs who bite and customers who might if their post isn't delivered on time. There are incomprehensible exhortations concerning franking – 'Customers *care* about the quality of cancellation' – which was news to me, and sinister instructions on dealing with (oh, shades of Le Carré) 'dead letters'. In truth, much more frightening are the gurneys, white plastic or brown wicker trolleys, universally used in the delivery offices but which look as if they would be more at home in a mortuary. Creepy things, with their squeaky, unoiled wheels. And all around the post itself, all those letters, parcels and cards to be sorted and sent out and through the alligator letterboxes.

Out in the country the mail is done by hand, at a speed so fast it looks like a conjuring trick: from bag, to gurney, to box and back to the bag again, out and ready to go, usually around the time when the early birds are contemplating stretching for their first worm. Work is done to music. I was never inside a delivery office without music spilling loudly from some high-pitched radio.

And then there was tea. Delivery offices usually had a canteen, immaculate as Robin Laing's Linlithgow Postbus and always a kettle, milk, sugar, tea bags and big mugs, generally full of a steaming hot brew, for the whole operation was fuelled by tea. But then so are posties. Not that things are altogether what they used to be on the tea line. Not only in the Post Offices but in the world outside it, where women work, leaving early for their jobs rather than keeping the teapot warm in the kitchen for the postie. Plus those homes where nothing warms until weekends or holidays.

Too little time now for the leisurely cup with the customers, although some of them try, especially those whose only daily visitor is the postie. Sometimes they offer more than tea. Steuart Murray in Kirkcudbright may happily gather sloes for his gin, but the elderly lady who tried to tempt him over her doorstep every morning with a pound note wrapped around a can of McEwan's was gently discouraged.

However there is always the flask that cheers if all else fails, although they told me even as they passed me a cup, that it didn't taste the same as a good strong fresh brew. Lucky Bill McIntosh with Mrs McLelland's cakes and best blend to look forward to every morning at his compulsory stop at Rannoch Station.

If the tea was a help, then the weather was not permitted to be a hindrance. I was lucky. That summer was more Indian than typically Scottish. Sunny and fresh and cloudfree, even although the trees were already on the turn and in the morning and it was not unknown for me to wipe a trace of frost from the windscreen. Every driver had a winter's tale to tell. In Dunoon Allan Gallacher regularly battles and wins against winds which screech to a hundred miles an hour. There is no time then for anyone to admire the view or watch buzzards swoop. Winter comes early and in some places never seems to lift its mantle entirely. When Stuart MacLeod-Slater and I took the bus up to Glenshee Ski Centre, there was already snow on the peaks. Stuart showed me the spot where he once leapt down from his Land Rover in a whiteout and disappeared into a drift: 'All they could see was my hat.' In winters up here drivers wear everything they can although one driver always removes his false teeth: 'The chattering noise when I'm cold gets me down.'

October and the snows are already lying on the crofts and cottages outside Braemar, at Linn of Dee.

In the delivery offices too there are always ranks of shovels for the winter snow – and maybe for the odd helping of manure for someone's summer roses. And of course to help rally drivers in distress. Keys, dully gleaming ranks of them, hang in the delivery offices with matching jangling clumps of them on the buses themselves to open and empty all the pillar boxes on their way. Sometimes, I was told, nasty things hide in mailboxes. Like the wasps' nest at Kirkandrews. Or there is the mystery of the postbox at Abingdon which houses a playing card, the seven of hearts. Who put it in there and why? John Doolan doesn't know anything other than that it's been there for years and he doesn't want to be the one who removes it.

The flags presented a puzzle too. I saw them on the way up from Pitlochry with Bill McIntosh as we crawled behind the tourist buses low-gearing their way to the panoramic delights of the Queen's View where Victoria once halted her carriage to stop and stare at the loch some 750 feet below. What were they? I asked Bill. What did all these scarves and old tea towels flowering bravely here and there from gateposts and farm ends mean? Trysts for lovers, cries for help, more dead letters? No, it was only the signal for Bill to stop and pick up something for the post. In places far away from a conventional box, the drivers will collect as well as deliver. I wondered if it would work elsewhere, in towns and cities, and imagined the sight of thousands of home-made flags fluttering from every door or window. But we like our pillar boxes, their solidity on our street corners a reassurance that some things do not change.

Some have lasted for years. For George VI still reigns happy and glorious in vermilion, and occasionally Queen Victoria does too. In scarlet relief, their initials live on after them, set deep into stone walls, and some at least will last for ever, like the box at Midlem down from Lilliesleaf which is officially protected for post and posterity by a preservation order.

The purpose of every postbox is not always immediately apparent, something discovered by two Americans travelling with Murdo down Loch Maree, where the post for the big house at Letterewe across the water is left a in small shack at the side of the road to be collected by boat. This ambiguity explains why Murdo regularly finds picnickers, fishermen and even sleeping campers inside, especially when it is wet. But only these two Americans have ever followed Murdo off the bus and waited quietly at the hut's door before politely asking if they too could use the loo please.

No proper pillar box is to be found at the end of Nigel Nice's run either, at the little harbour where the boat to Soay stops to pick up its mail from an old parked van. Nigel once found half a dozen hens waiting inside to be ferried across. Fortunately they were not in a laying mood.

Some boxes are very grand indeed or at least have grand associations. The Duke of Roxburghe at Floors Castle pays the Royal Mail to collect his estate workers' mail, and although the box itself is rather ordinary – green, dull wood fixed into a stable wall – the setting is from another time. Here, unlike neglected, empty Castle Grant, Floors still flourishes in the grand manner, surrounded by its policies, gardens and glittering glasshouses, its farms and stables with well-maintained cottages behind its high stone perimeter walls. Upstairs and Downstairs living on, neither quite as feudal nor as great as it once was, but still an old family, supporting and providing for itself and its

own extended family. The duke, I was told, had recently taken a new duchess.

'The last one,' opined Jim, 'was a very nice lady indeed. But,' he went on, cannily and ever mindful of my nose and notebook, 'I am sure this one will be a very nice lady too.'

Jim Brodie drove me on my last postbus journey back to Kelso, past the old shop fronts, their hanging baskets outside dripping in the rain. As we left the bus it was time for another cup of tea and for me to reflect on my brief initiation into the ways of another Scotland. I enjoyed those dying summer days as I travelled with the postbus regulars, when I wore out ten notebooks and perhaps as many people's patience. But I thank them for their tolerance. And their humour – invariably good.

I saw too many early hours of the morning: posties and delivery offices, I learned, start up well before the dawn chorus. I also learned it is unwise to have too many cups of coffee for breakfast, and to forgo the ever-preferred tea. Postbuses do not come with lavatories attached. I learned many other things along the way, including the best way to make sloe gin and friends of recalcitrant collies. Above all, I learned that the postbus is an inheritance to be cherished and that many lives would be the less, much less, without it.

The old stage coaches would have little difficulty in recognising the carefully preserved shopfronts and buildings in the centre of Kelso. Only the pillarbox has changed.

POSTBUS ROUTES IN SCOTLAND
WITH DATE OF INTRODUCTION

DUNBAR - INNERWICK	4.6.1968	TIMSGARRY - CALLNISH/STORNOWAY	5.4.1977
LUING - circular	3.5.1976	THORNHILL - MONIAIVE	28.9.1973
ELGOL - BROADFORD	17.4.1972	CRIANLARICH - KILLIN	23.5.1977
HALKIRK - ALTNABREAC	19.7.1976	BOWMORE - PORT ASKAIG	1.10.1973
LOCHMADDY - NEWTON SOLLAS	16.6.1972	HUNTLY - LUMSDEN	2.5.1977
BIGGAR - NEWBIGGING	17.8.1976	BOWMORE - PORT ASKAIG	1.10.1973
MELROSE - LILLIESLEAF	28.8.1972	INVERARAY - DALMALLY	7.5.1977
DUNBLANE - BRACO/LANGSIDE	21.9.1976	PORTNAHAVEN - ISLAY	1.10.1973
SCOURIE - ELPHIN	15.9.1972	DUNS - ABBEY/ST BATHANS	18.8.1977
KIRKCUDBRIGHT - GATEHOUSE OF FLEET	25.10.1976	KYLE - LETTERFEARN	7.11.1973
CUPAR - PEAT INN	4.12.1972	PEEBLES - MANORHEAD	16.8.1977
KIRKCUDBRIGHT - LENNOX PLUNTON	25.10.1976	ANSTRUTHER - ARNCROACH	3.1.1974
TIGHARRY - BALINVANICH AIRPORT	1.12.1972	BRODICK - BLACKWATERFOOT	30.8.1977
INVERGORDON - KILDERMORIE	18.10.1976	ABERFELDY - GLENLYON-LUBREOCH	3.1.1974
SKERRAY - TONGUE/MELVICH	29.1.1973	BRODICK - PIRNMILL	30.8.1977
BIRNAM - ABERFELDY	25.10.1976	ABERFELDY - LAWERS/BRIDGEND	3.1.1974
NAIRN - GLENFERNESS	28.2.1973	BRODICK - SHANNOCHIE	30.8.1977
HAWICK - CRAIK	15.11.1976	ARDGAY - THE CRAIGS	20.6.1974
LOCKERBIE - HIGHTAE	23.4.1993	CASTLEBAY - EOLIGARRY (circular)	17.8.1972
ANNAN - POWFOOT	17.11.1975	DURNESS - LAIRG (ALTNAHARRA)	20.6.1974
LOCKERBIE - ST ANNES	21.04.1973	BIGGAR - LANARK	19.9.1977
DOLLAR - GLENDEVON	29.11.1976	INVERNESS - TOMATIN	20.6.1974
ALLIGIN - KINLOCHEWE	2.6.1973	BRODICK - KILMORY	16.1.1978
PITLOCHRY - DALNASPITAL	22.11.1976	HADDINGTON - GARVALD	25.6.1974
SCOURIE - KYLESTROME	1.6.1973	DENNY - FINTRY	10.3.1978
KELSO - SMAILHOLME	6.12.1976	WEST LINTON - ROMANO BRIDGE	28.8.1974
STRATHCONON - MUIR OF ORD	2.6.1973	BALLATER - LIN OF DEE	27.3.1978
BRESSAY - circular	6.12.1976	CASTLE DOUGLAS - CORSOCK	29.8.1974
ARDGAY - STRATHOYKEL	21.7.1973	ROUSAY (circular)	24.3.1978
KINROSS - RUMBLING BRIDGE	7.2.1977	CASTLE DOUGLAS - MOSSDALE	29.8.1974
LOCHINVER - DRUMBEG	2.7.1973	DALMALLY - BRIDGE OF ORCHY	20.3.1978
BIGGAR - DUNEATON	22.3.1977	WEST CALDER - TARBRAX	22.8.1974
BETTYHILL - KINBRACE	10.8.1973	BLAIRGOWRIE - GLENSHEE	31.3.1978
BERNERA - CALLANISH	4.4.1977	ROGART - SCIBERSCROSS	30.9.1974
BIGGAR - TWEEDSMUIR	11.8.1973	STRATHAVEN - DUNGAVEL	24.4.'978

KIRRIEMUIR - GLEN CLOVA	2.9.1974	ARNISDALE - KYLE	20.10.1975
KELSO - HASSINGTON	5.6.1978	HUNTLY - CLATT	8.10.1984
KIRRIEMUIR - GLEN PROSEN	2.9.1974	LOCHMADDY - SIDINISH/BALESHARE	27.10.1975
ARMADALE - MELVICH/THURSO	5.6.1978	HUNTLY - CABRACH	7.1.1985
HAWICK - BONCHESTER	15.10.1974	KILLIN - CALLANDER	24.11.1975
CUPAR - BIRKHALL	31.7.1978	ROGART - MUIE/LAIRG	18.11.1987
KELSO - STICHILL	15.10.1974		
CUPAR - BIRKHALL	31.7.1978	LOCKERBIE - WATERBECK	17.11.1975
MELROSE - MAXTON	7.1.1975	GAIRLOCH - MELVAIG/REDPOINT	19.9.1988
CUPAR - NEWBURGH	31.7.1978	DALWHINNIE - DRUMMIN	5.11.1975
ABERFOYLE - KINLOCHARD	8.1.1975	JOHN O'GROATS - WICK	13.1.1989
DUNOON - TIGHNABRUICH	3.7.1978	KINBRACE - MELVICH	3.11.1975
APPLECROSS - SHIELDAIG	27.1.1975	PITLOCHRY - RANNOCH STATION	4.1.1989
CUPAR - NEWBURGH-LETHAM	1.8.1978	SCARINISH - TIREE	27.11.1975
INVERNESS - GORTHLECK	18.2.1975	INVERGARRY - FORT AUGUSTUS	19.6.1989
ABERFELDY - KENMORE	28.9.1978	TARBERT - SKIPNESS	17.11.1975
SHIELDAIG - KISHORN	27.2.1975	BLAIRGOWRIE - GLEN ISLA	5.6.1989
DUNVEGAN - GLENDALE	27.11.1978	ANNAN - CRECA	19.1.1976
KELSO - ROXBURGH	25.3.1975		
DUNVEGAN - WATERNISH	27.11.1978	BALLACHULISH - FORT WILLIAM-GLEN ETIVE	16.9.1991
SELKIRK - ASHKIRK	6.3.1975	GLENLUCE - NEWLUCE	20.1.1976
LINLITHGOW - BLACKNESS	8.1.1979	DURNESS - LAIRG	10.8.1992
LEVEN - GILSTON	26.3.1975	LOCKERBIE - CORRIE	19.1.1976
GOREBRIDGE - MOORFOOT	26.3.1979	LOCHINVER - LAIRG	10.8.1992
DINGWALL - DOCHARTY	10.3.1975	ABOYNE - LOGIE-COLDSTONE	26.1.1976
TALMINE - TONGUE/LAIRG	19.11.1979	FORT WILLIAM - GARVAN	2.11.1992
GRANTOWN ON SPEY - LOCHINDORB	4.3.1975	FORRES - BRAEMORAY	19.1.1976
SANDAY - BROUGHTON	23.1.1980	INVERARAY - LOCHGILPHEAD	20.12.1993
CASTLE DOUGLAS - AUCHENCAIRN	6.6.1975	LAIDE - ACHNASHEEN	5.1.1976
SANDAY - LADY/RUSNESS	23.1.1980	DUNS - CRANSHAW	9.5.1994
DRUMNADROCHIT - GROTAIG/ACHTEMARACK	2.6.1975	BALFRON - FINTRY	9.2.1976
DUNS - LONGFORMACUS	11.3.1982	LISMORE - circular	13.6.1994
KYLE - PLOCTON/STROMEFERRY	11.9.1975	INVERGARRY - KINLOCHOURNE	2.2.1976
BANCHORY - BALLATER	2.8.1982	COLONSAY - circular	16.2.1976
LAIRG - ATLASS/ROSEHALL	9.9.1975	CALLANDER - TROSSACHS	30.3.1976
BANCHORY - LUMPHANAN	2.8.1982	NEWTONMORE - KINLOCHLAGGAN	8.3.1976
POOLEWE - COVE	12.9.1975	ABERFOYLE - INVERSNAID	21.4.1976
THURSO - WICK	22.11.1982		

111